is fair of face...

Photos of
JILL
on the occasion of her 80th birthday
3rd August, 2022

On Monday 3rd August 1942 the best person in the world was born. Gillian Ann Chapman. Not only is she still the wisest, calmest, most selfless, and most Chapmanly-humorous person to walk the earth, this book of photos will prove beyond all reasonable doubt that she's the most beautiful too.

Gillian's convinced any creativity that might on occasion be demonstrated by a daughter or grandson has nothing whatsoever to do with her... *I have no imagination* is a regular assertion of hers. Even though her family keep telling her she's a brilliant writer. So included in this book are some examples of her work from when Jacqueline and Sara-Jane were young.

BEDTIME SONG

to the tune of 'non piu andrai', Le Nozze di Figaro

Say 'goodnight' to your dear old father
Or to Daddy, if you would rather.
He's been busy so he's all of a lather...
Say 'goodnight' to the silly old fool!

After that say 'goodnight' to your mother,
Then turn around and say 'goodnight' to each other.
Say 'goodnight' to the cat and the rabbit...
But you'd better not let this become a habit!

MY JILLIE

Who would have thought, 56 years ago, that the young lady I met in the romantic setting of the photocopying booth at Vauxhall Motors' publicity studio would still be at my side today at the grand old age of 80. Yes, we met in T-Block at the huge Vauxhall factory in Kimpton Road, Luton and, having mastered the 'Copycat' copying process, we spent our lunch breaks together and formed a bond. Being a shy young man with a serious lack of self confidence, it took enormous courage for me to ask her out. Our first date found us at a pub in Barton-le-Cley enjoying a drink or two.

After that there was no stopping us – we were an item! Before long we were getting to know one another's families and venturing further afield in my old VW van – even up to 'Bonnie Scotland' where, in May 1967, I plucked up the courage to propose marriage. That all happened on a beautiful day on the Isle of Skye and I was very happy when she said 'yes'. We set the date of September 16th 1967 for the big day.

Fifty six years on, here we are celebrating another great landmark, having both become octogenarians. Like any couple we've had a few struggles at times but by and large we've survived and we can now look back on a pretty successful and rewarding time together. Our two daughters, Jacqueline and Sara-Jane, have done us proud and continue to help us as we get older – without them we would certainly find life difficult.

Come to think of it, Jillie deserves credit too for the way she's put up with me over the years. As I'm a lorry enthusiast or, if you like, a 'truck nut', she's had to put up with a lot. Some wives are 'golf widows' while others are forced to spend time attending sporting events that might bore them to tears. I have subjected poor Jillie and the girls to lorry shows, suffering the noise and discomfort of travelling thousands of miles in old diesel powered eight-wheelers – how they put up with me and my hobby over the years I shall never know.

Having put all the active lorry show involvement behind us we can now enjoy a rather more sedate lifestyle these days. Looking back once more we haven't done too badly as we work as a team. We had a successful few years attending lorry rallies with our sales stand, flogging truck pictures and other memorabilia while we've had an equally successful business in truck journalism – I write the articles while Jillie does the typing. She often says that's the only reason I asked her to marry me – because she's a professional typist!

I can't emphasize enough how much Jillie and the girls mean to me. I count myself very lucky that Jillie found it difficult to operate that old Copycat machine! We've had a great time together and, Deo volente, we have a good many more years ahead of us. We are, after all, young-thinking octogenarians. We'll keep doing the cryptic crosswords and hope for the best.

Happy 80th Birthday Jillie and Many Happy Returns of the Day!

From Peter, July 25th 2022.

Wasn't it grand
To sit in the sand
And do a little wee-wee?
Nobody knew...
Because it soaked through!
Sometimes sand is very handy.

© Jill Davies

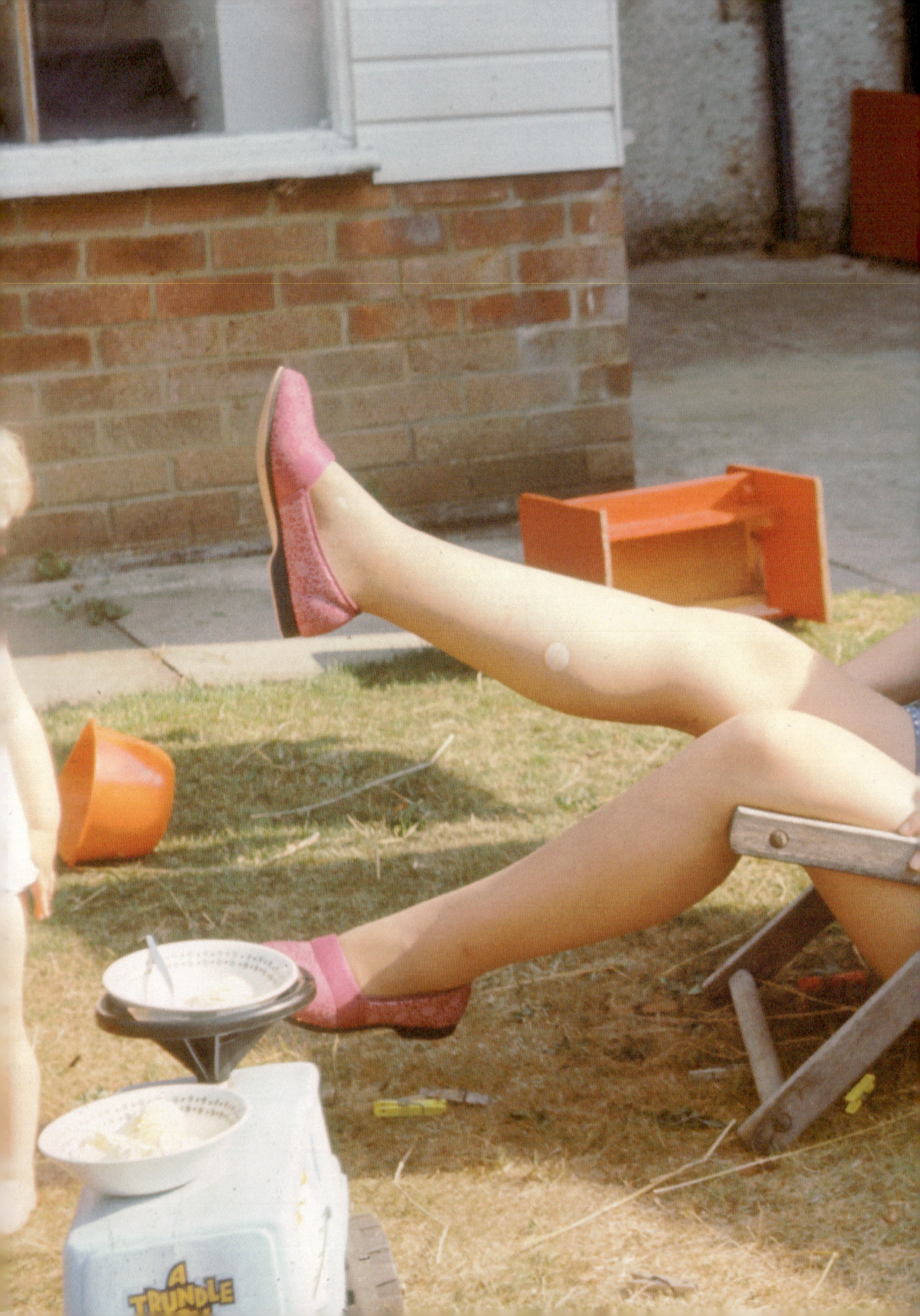
A
TRUNDLE

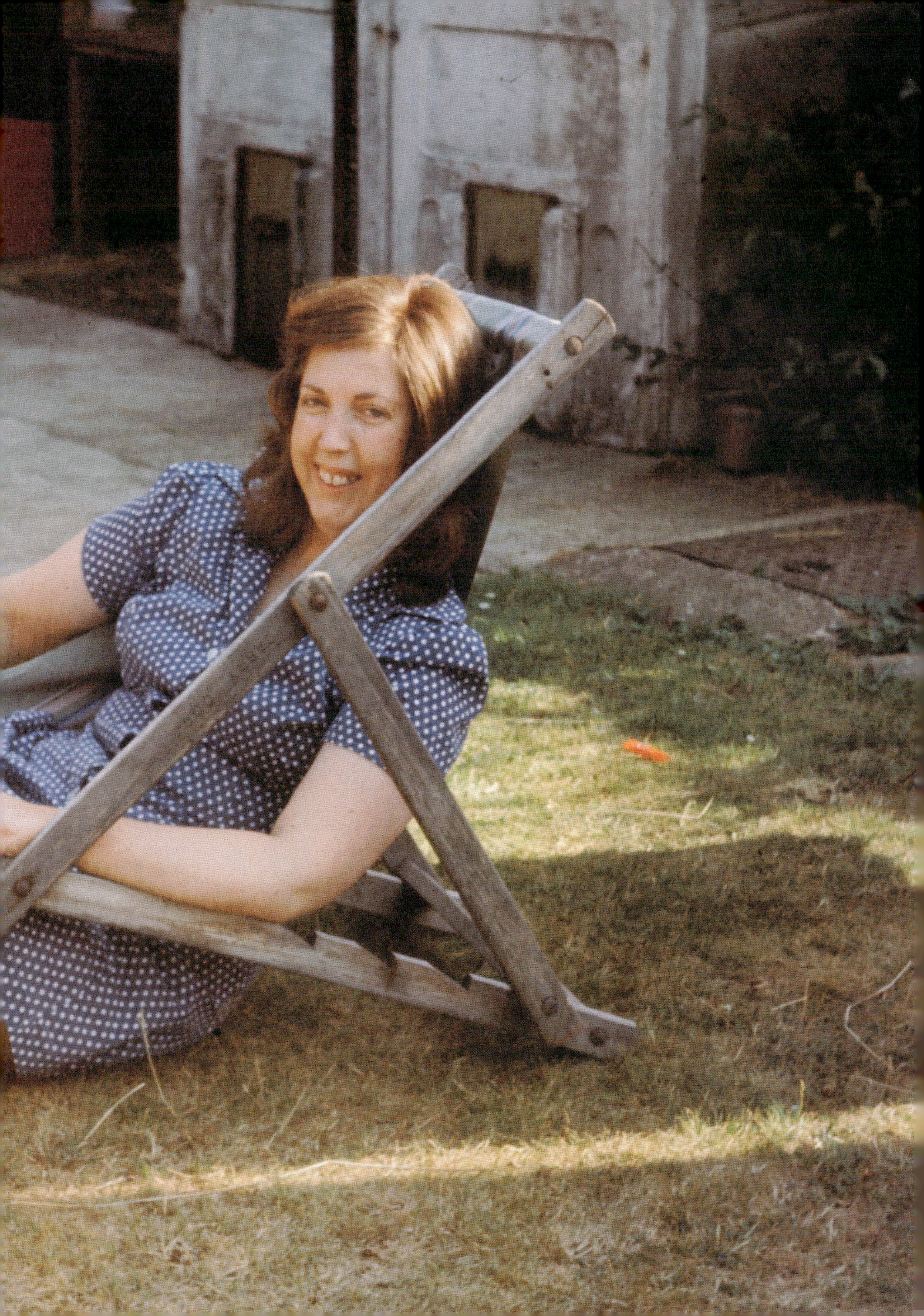

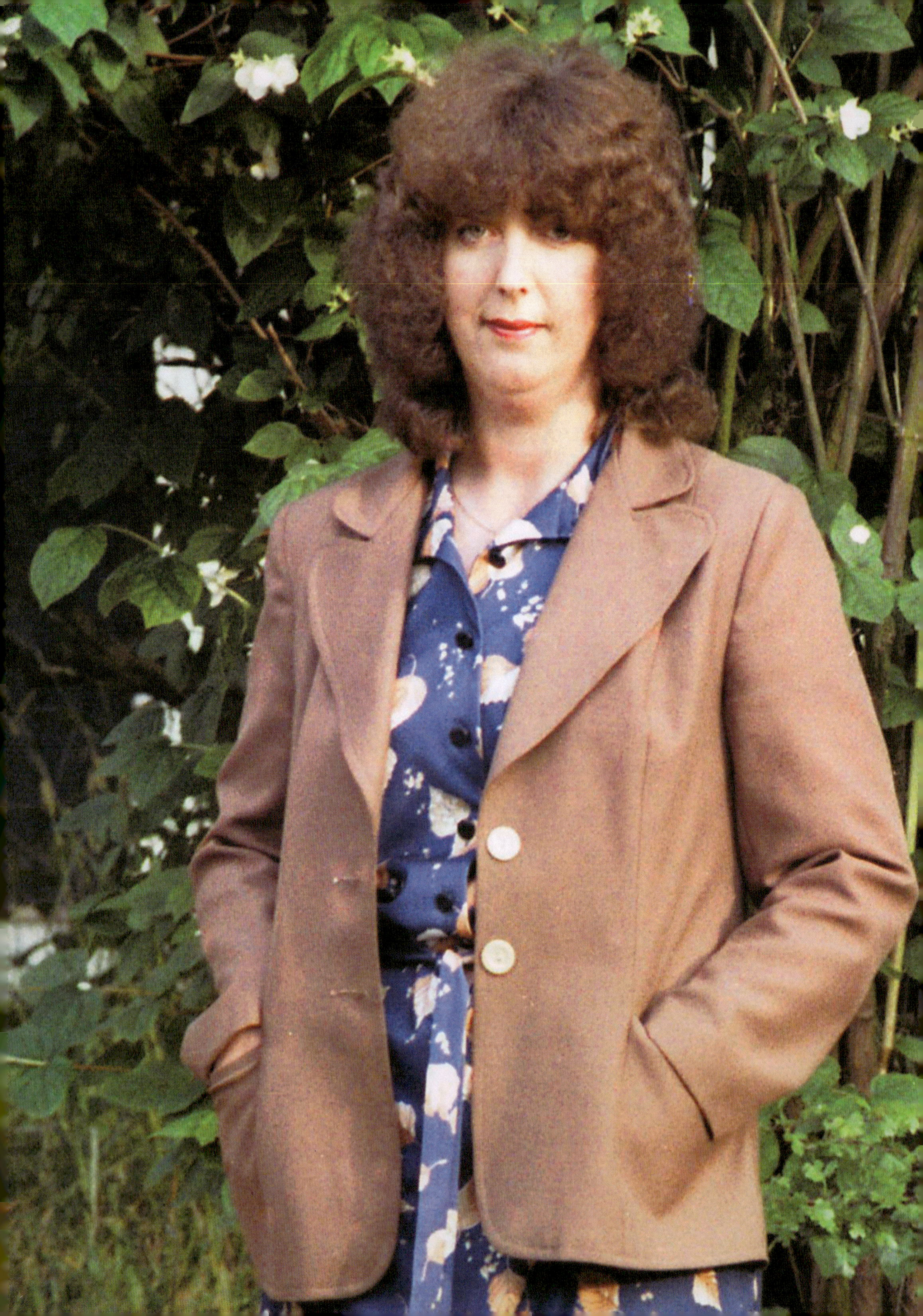

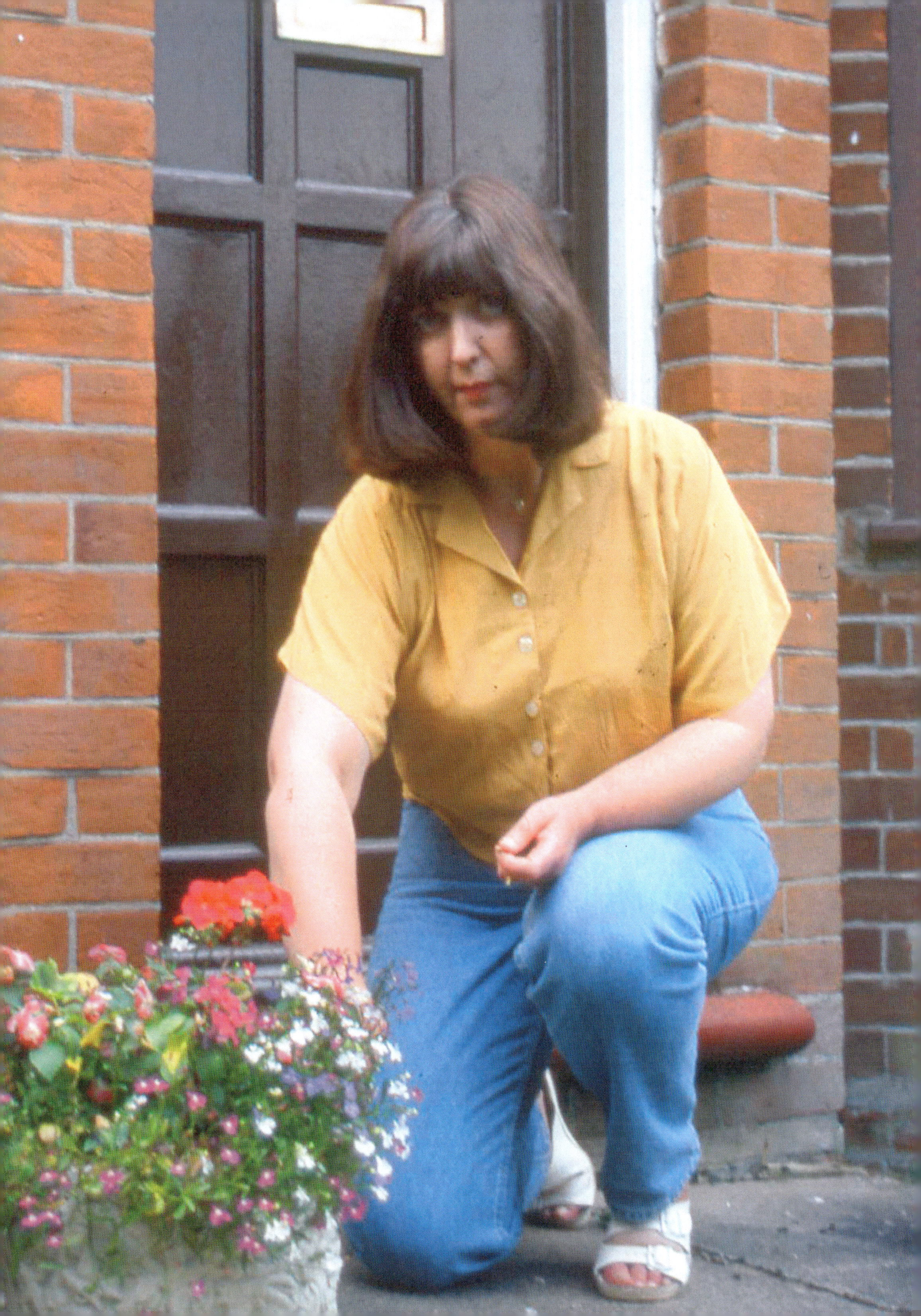

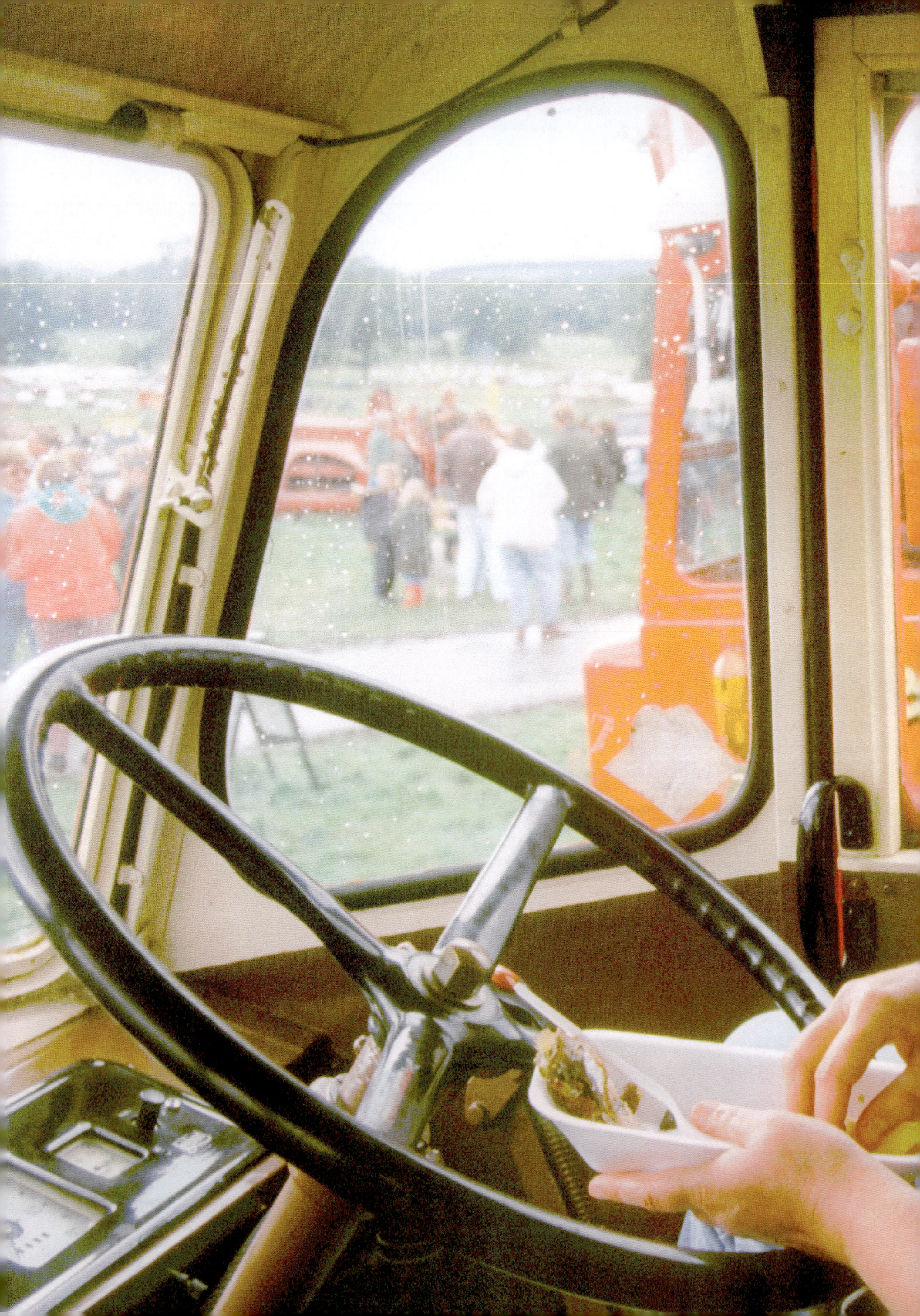

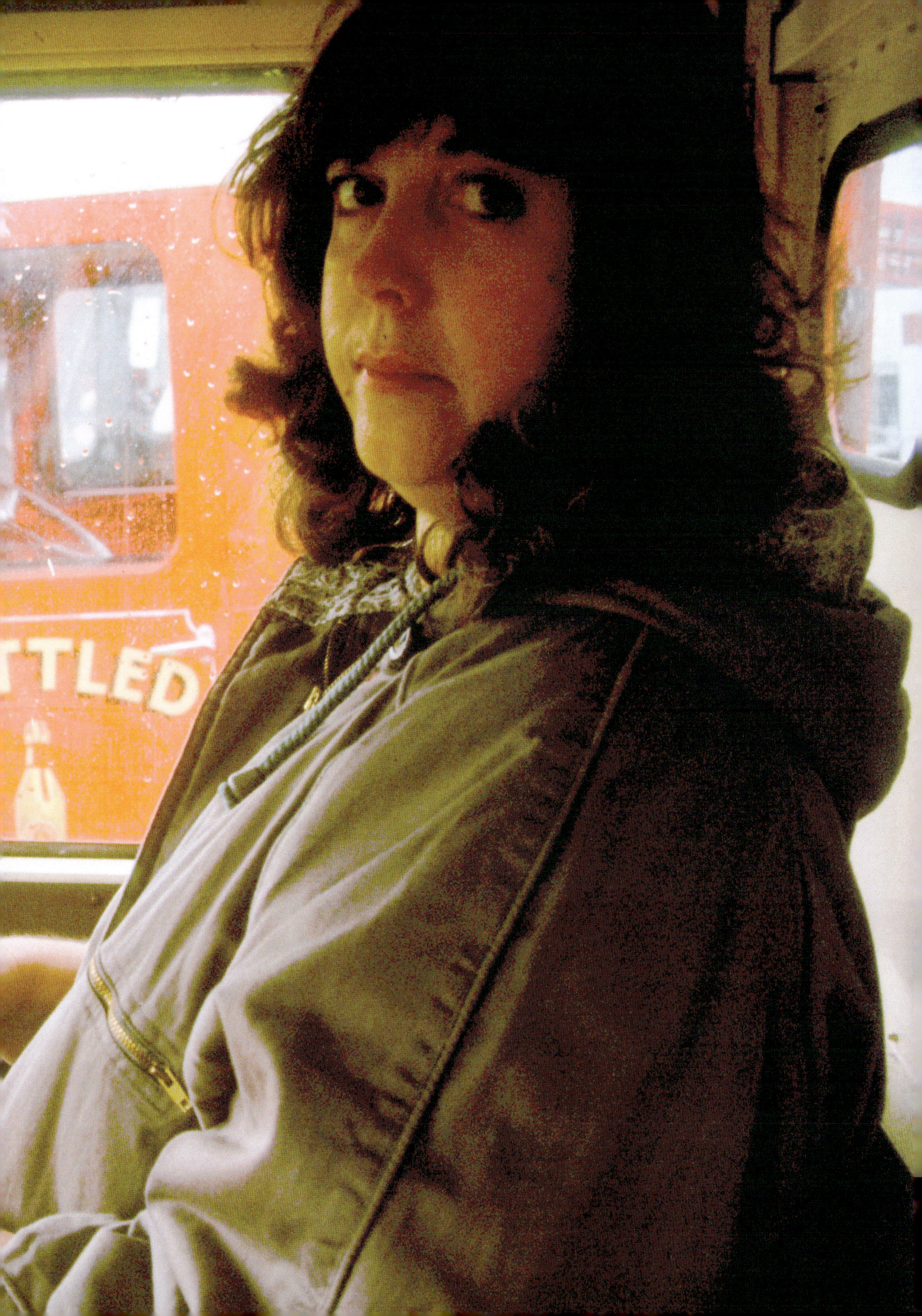
TTLED

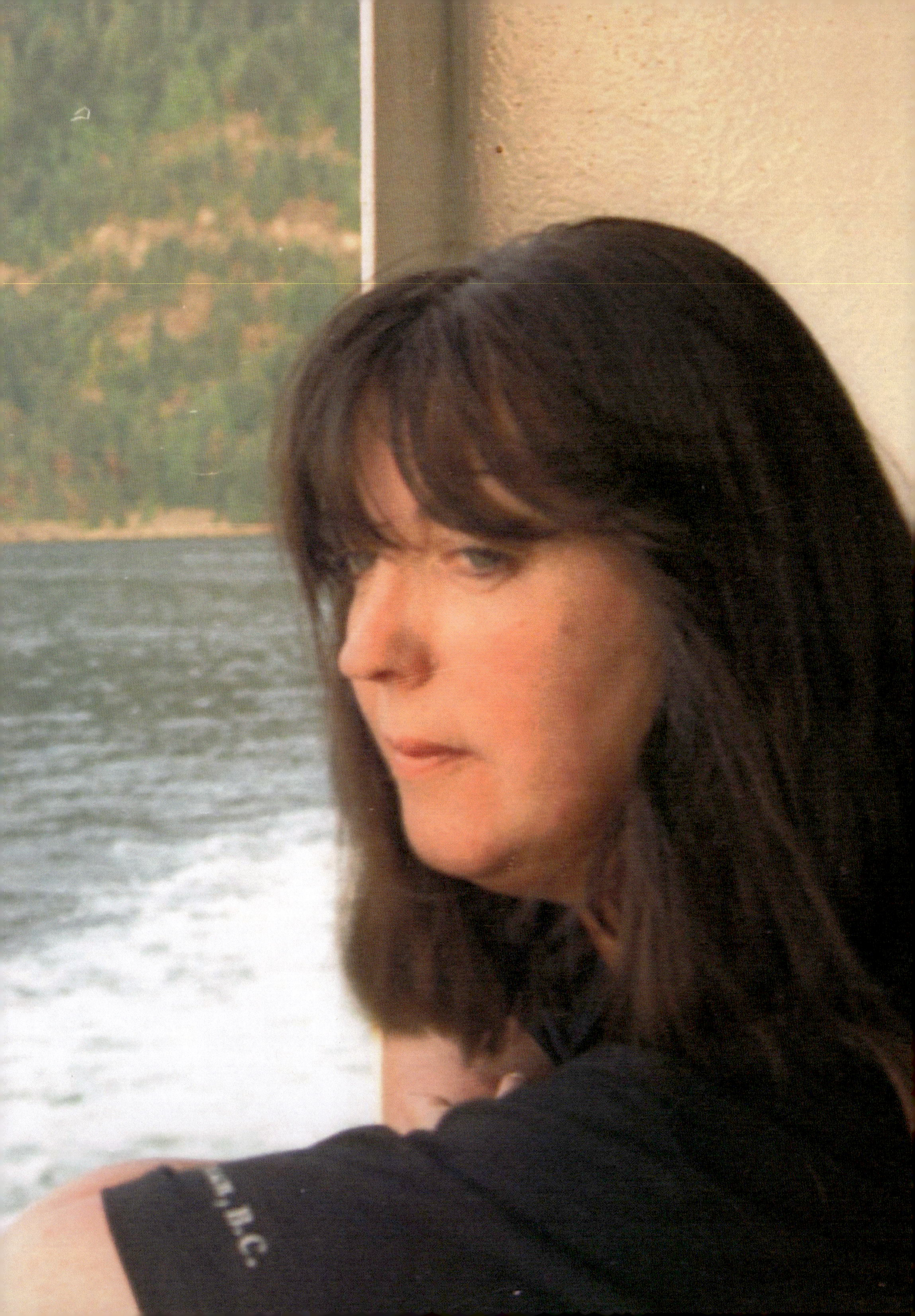
B.C.

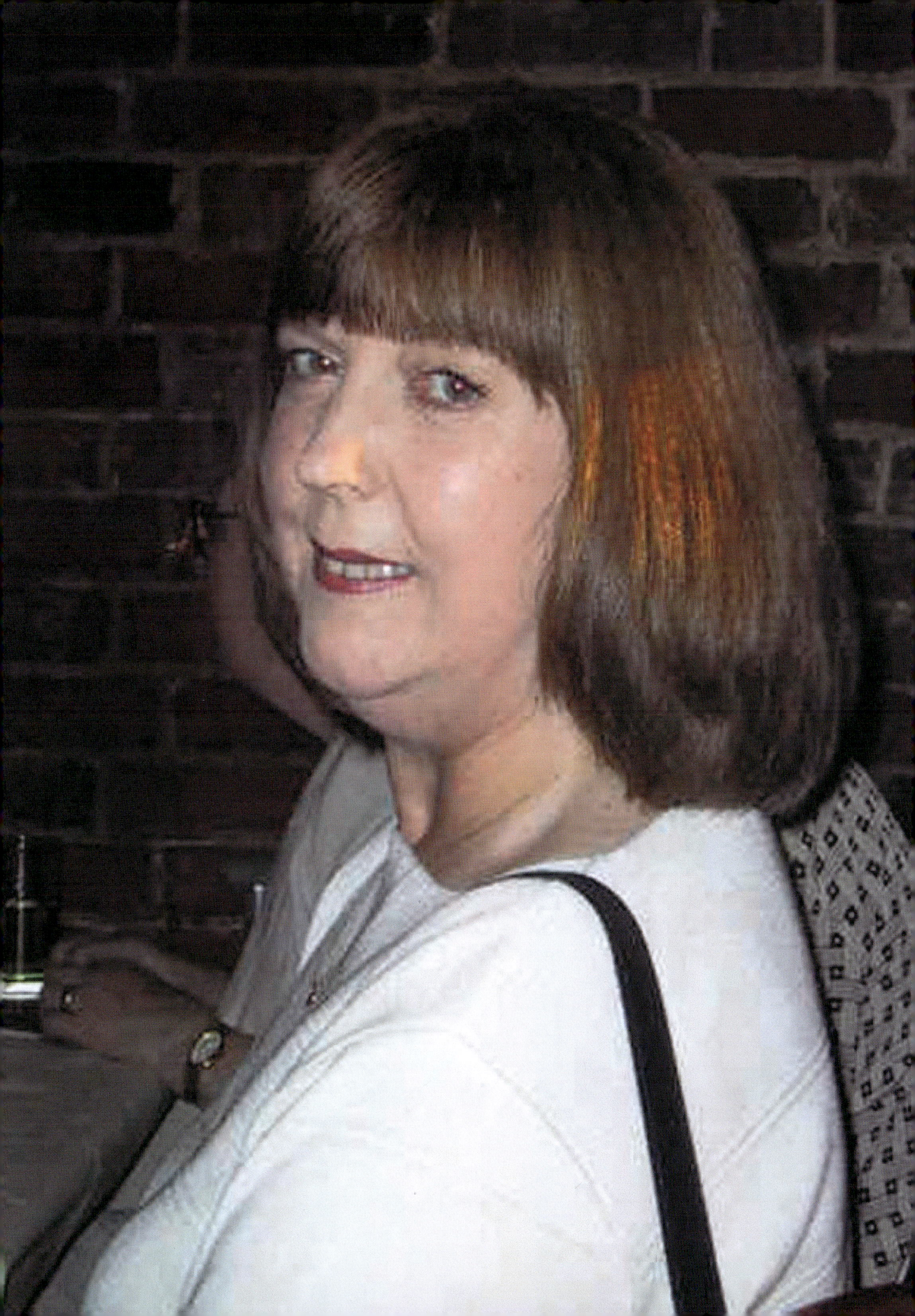

TO MUM, MUMMA, MATER

There has not been a single day in my life when you have not been there. Rather aptly, at the time of writing, you have been my mum for 17,717 days. For more than 425,000 hours you have been on hand. Reachable. An unwavering support. I wonder how many words we've spoken in that time, how many times we've laughed. It's impossible to say. But it's easy to say how many cross words we have spoken, how many times we have argued, because the answer is: none.

You taught me how to write my name, you taught me how to do simple sums. My happy memories of doing things revolve around you and the little things you thought of, like playing squares and stitching little pictures. Whether you realise it or not, it's because of you that I love birds, and nature, and the simple things. All the things that make me happy today.

Thank you for being so selfless for all these years. Thank you for never losing your temper with me. Thank you for making room on your lap for me when I was little. Thank you for reading all those bedtime stories. Thank you for showing me how to make an omelette. Thank you for your advice, for your quiet, calm influence. Thank you for always being fair. Thank you for being so wickedly funny, and for always taking an interest. Thank you for loving me, despite all my shortcomings and all the things I haven't been able to do. Thank you for being my mum. You couldn't be any better.

This still says it all, and it always will:

All the things you do mean more than words can say
Tumbling, falling, I hear you calling, and I know you're on your way.
I never won your love, you loved me from the start
I don't need to put a name to what you put in my heart.
And I would gladly run and catch the sun if you were feeling cold
Wish I could cast a spell to stop us growing old; you mean the world to me
And when I've made mistakes, you've always understood.
When I can't be all I should be, you know my soul is good.
I love you with my heart, that's all I need to say
I don't need to put a name to what you give me today.
Wish I could write a tune to catch the moon, put silver in your sight
You will always be my only guiding light; you mean the world to me.

That you do, Mum. That you do.
Happy 80th Birthday.
Love Sara-Jane xxx

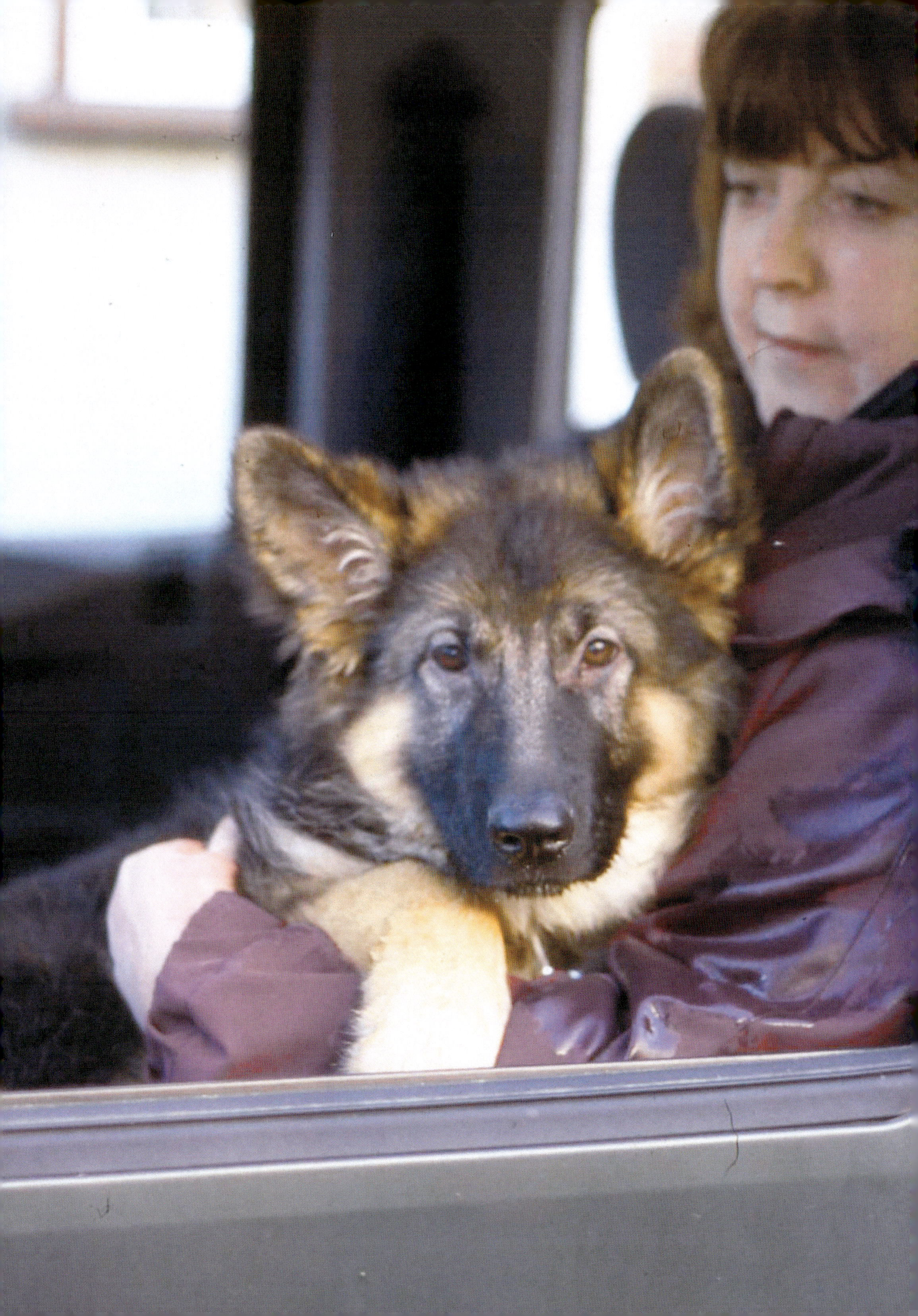

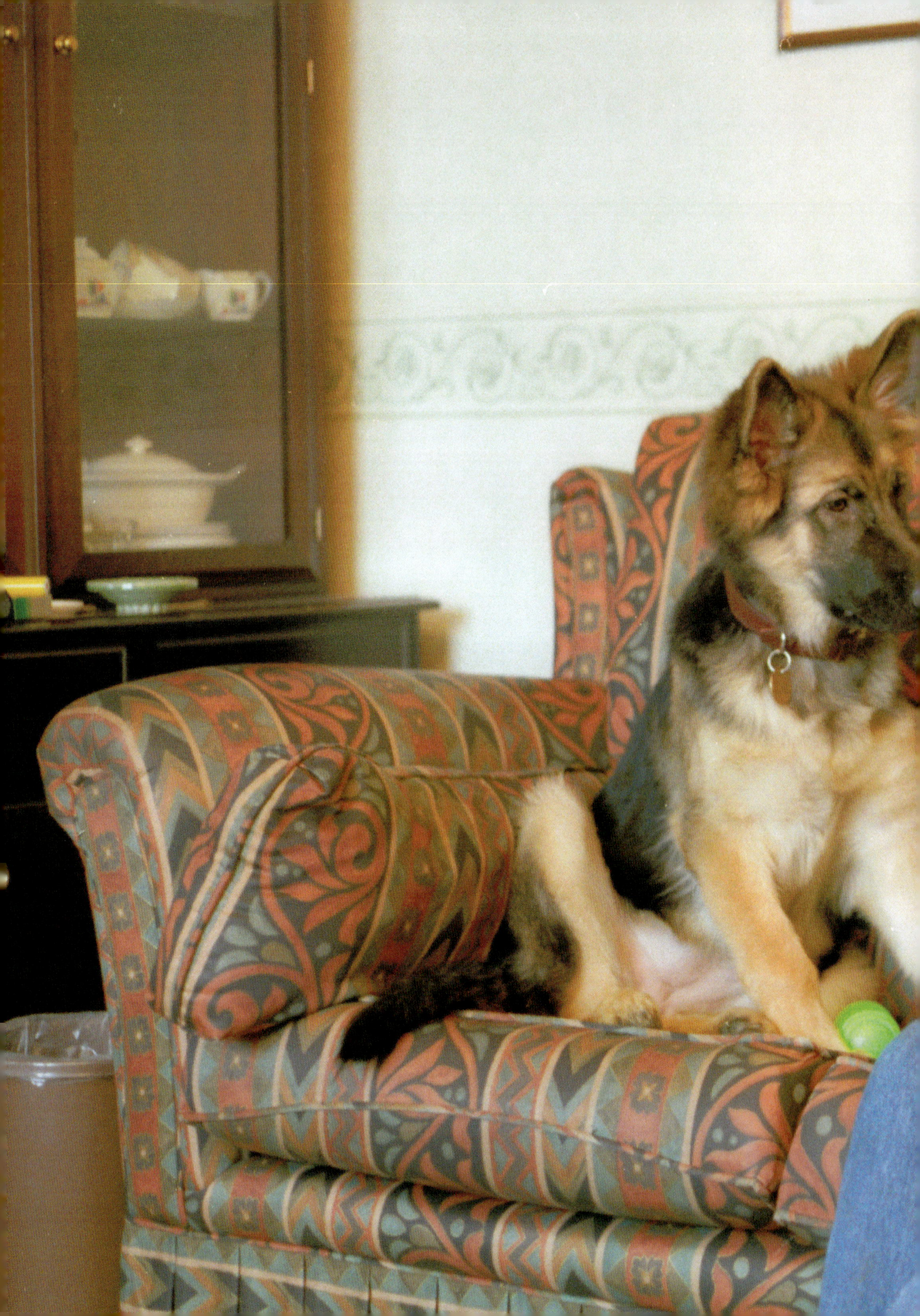

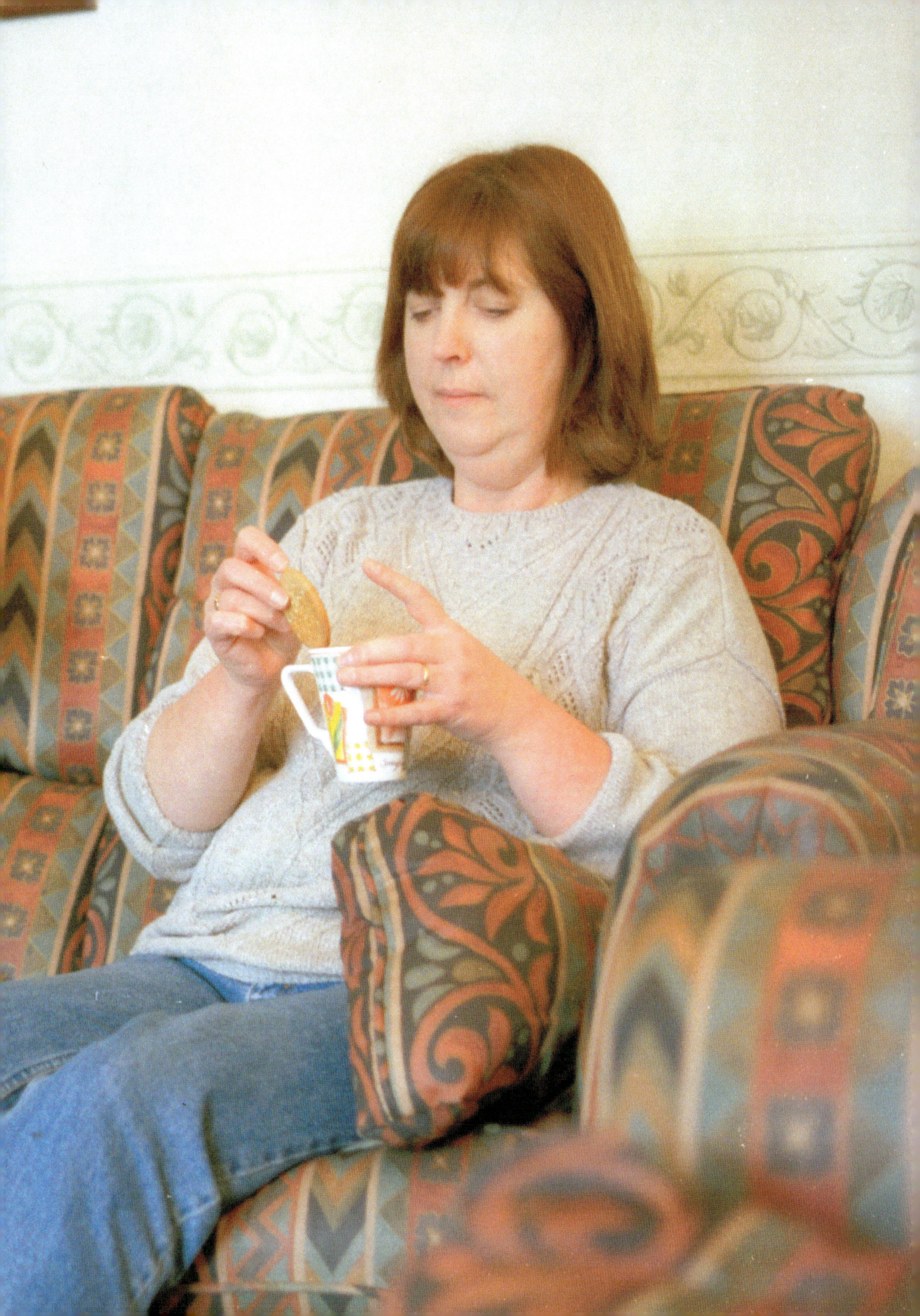

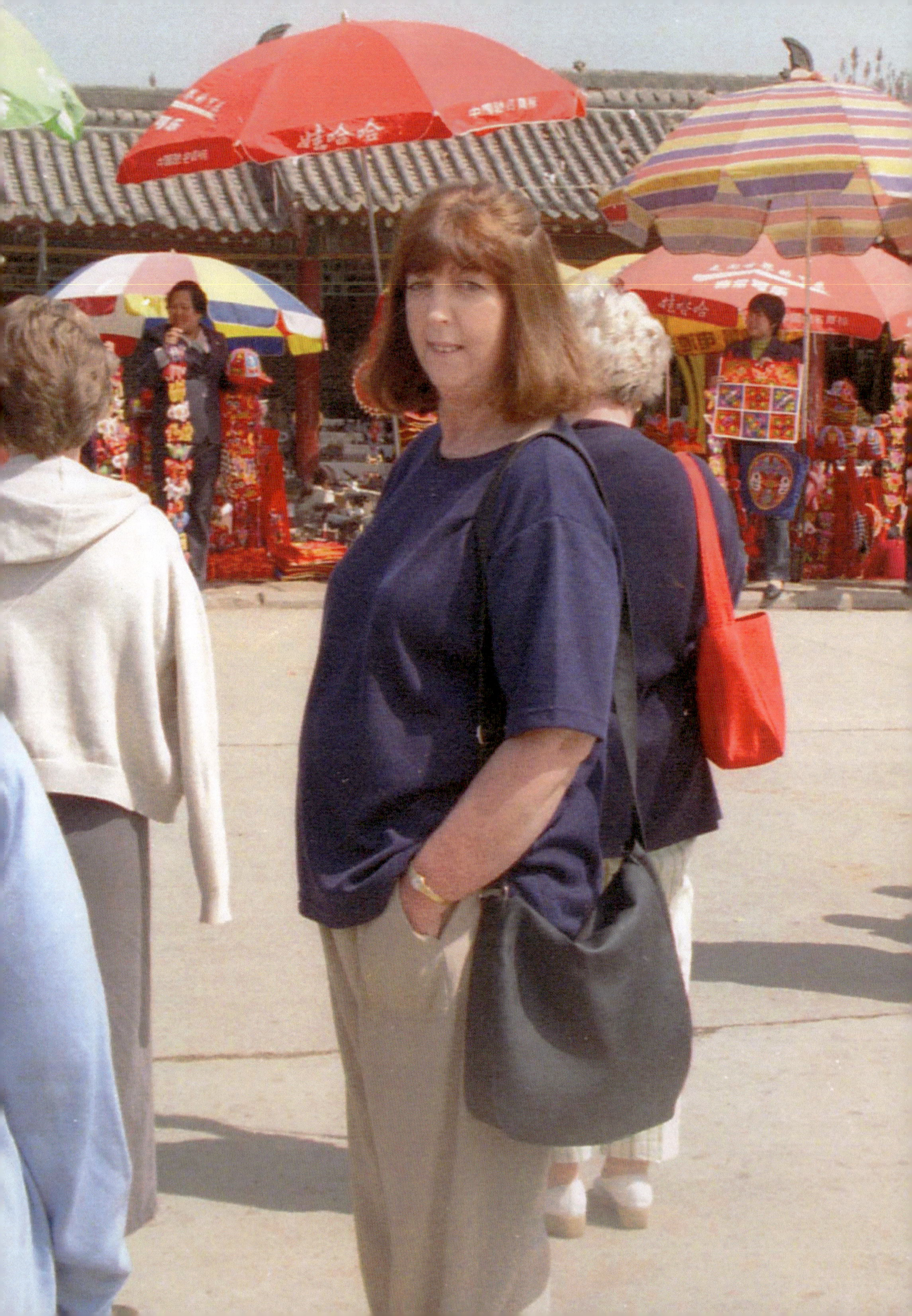
娃哈哈
娃哈哈

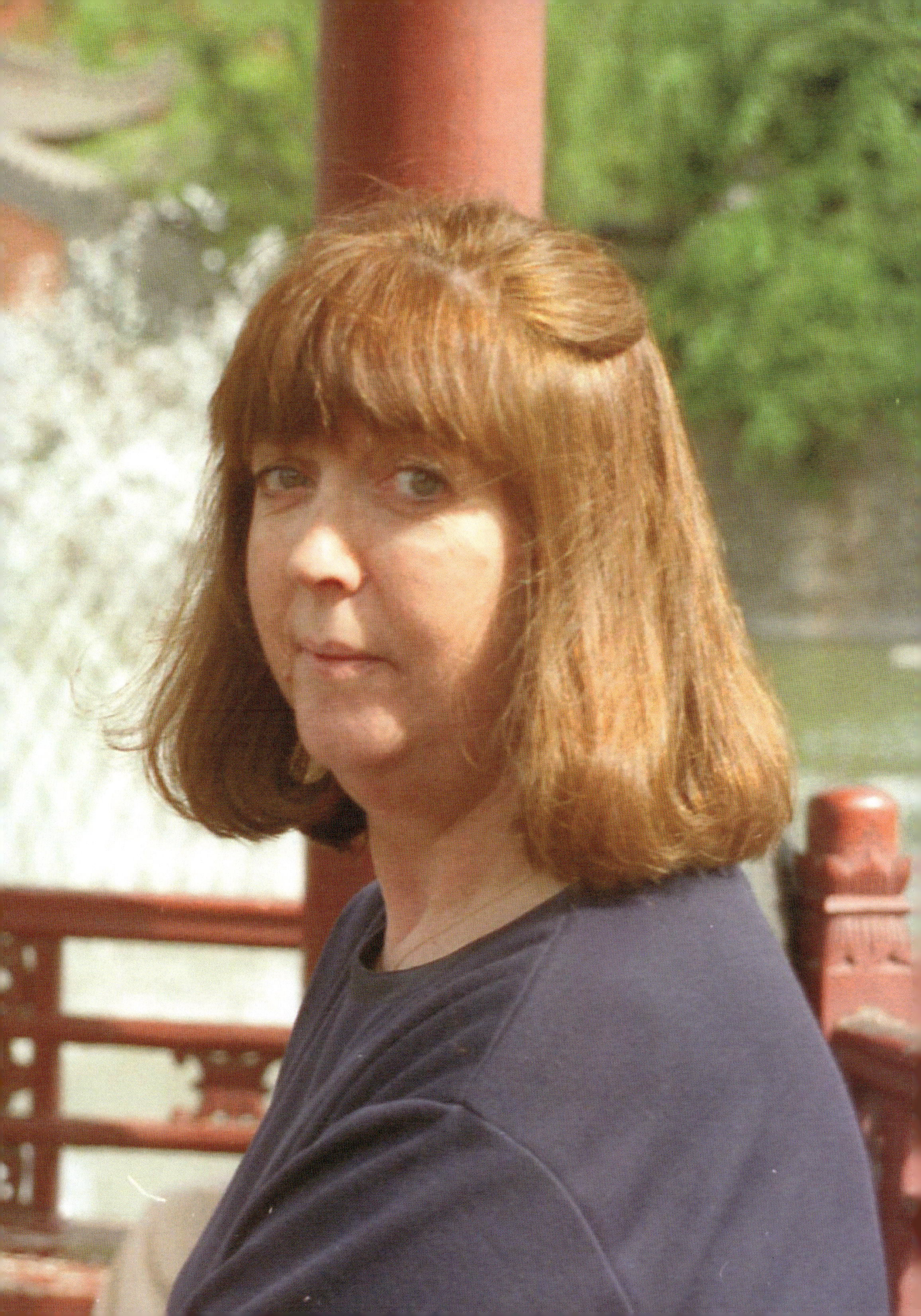

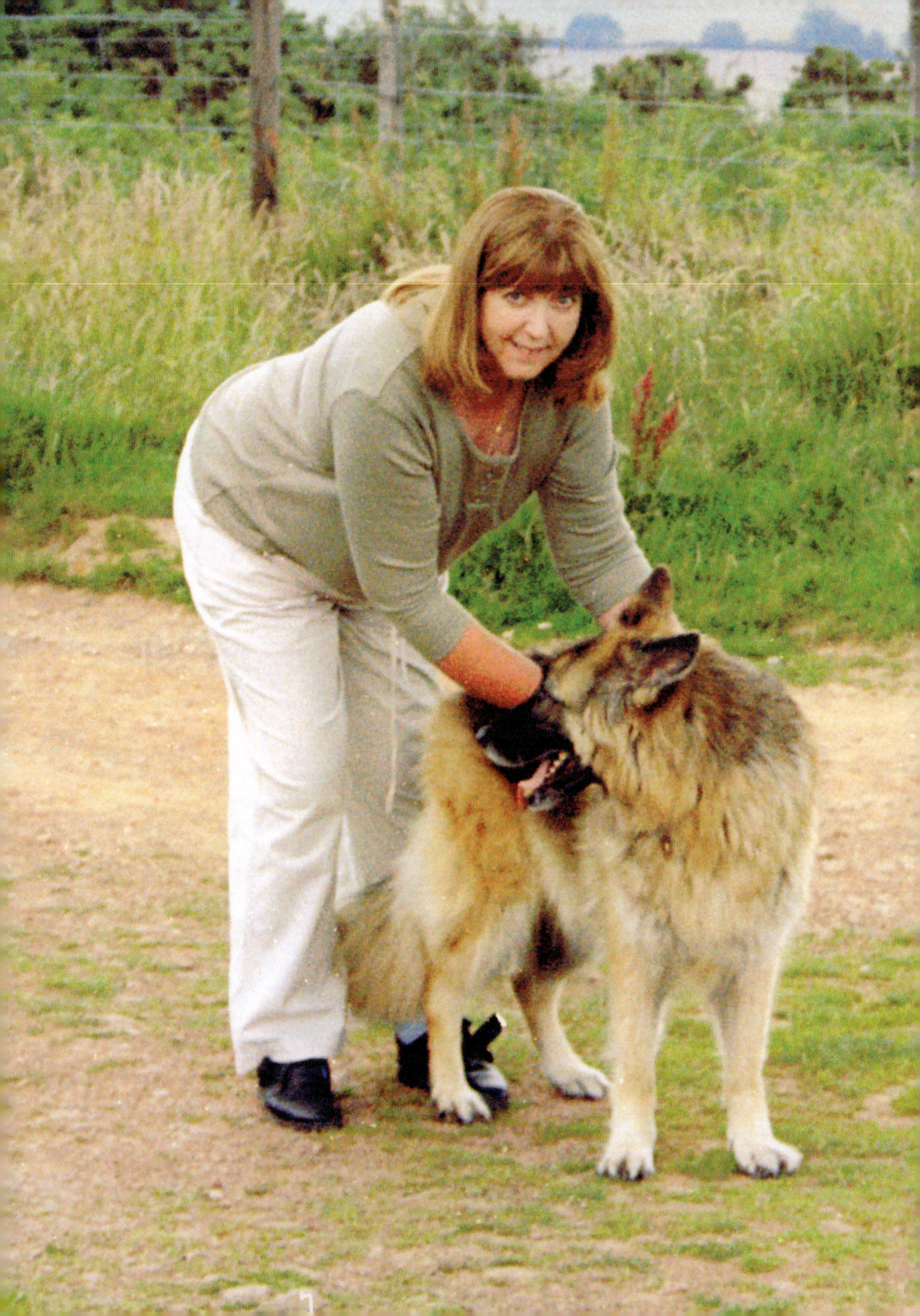

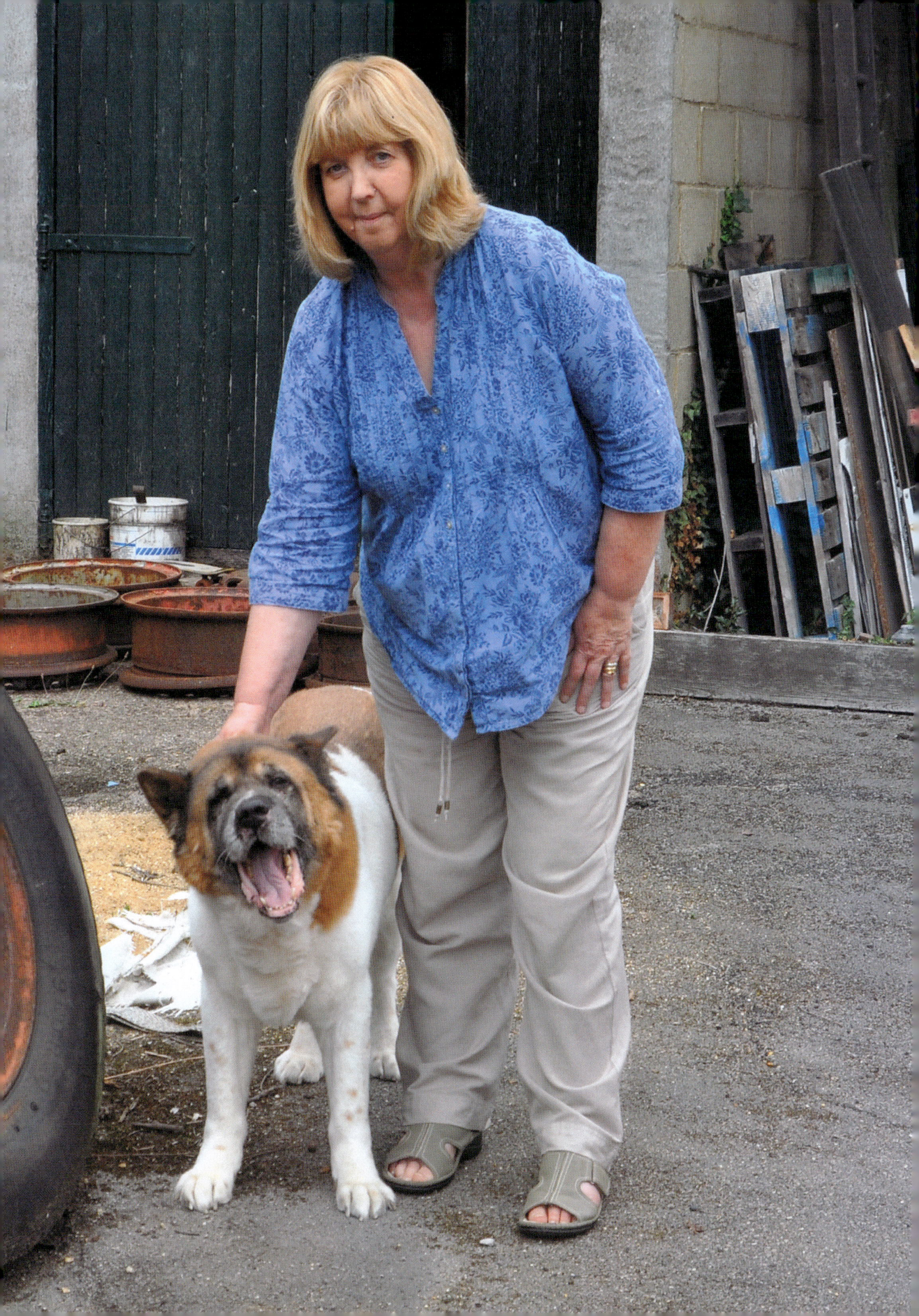

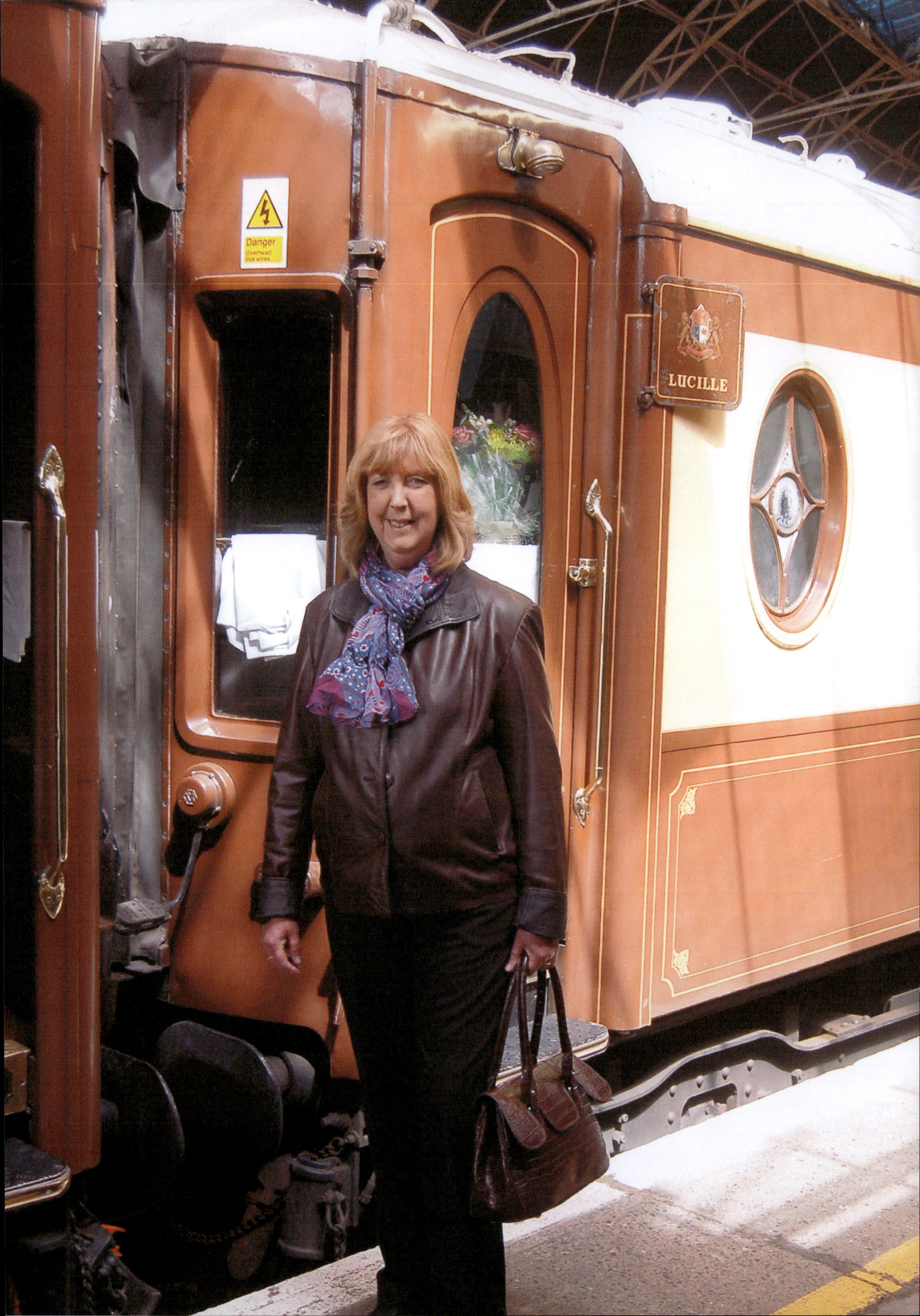
Danger
Overhead
live wires
LUCILLE

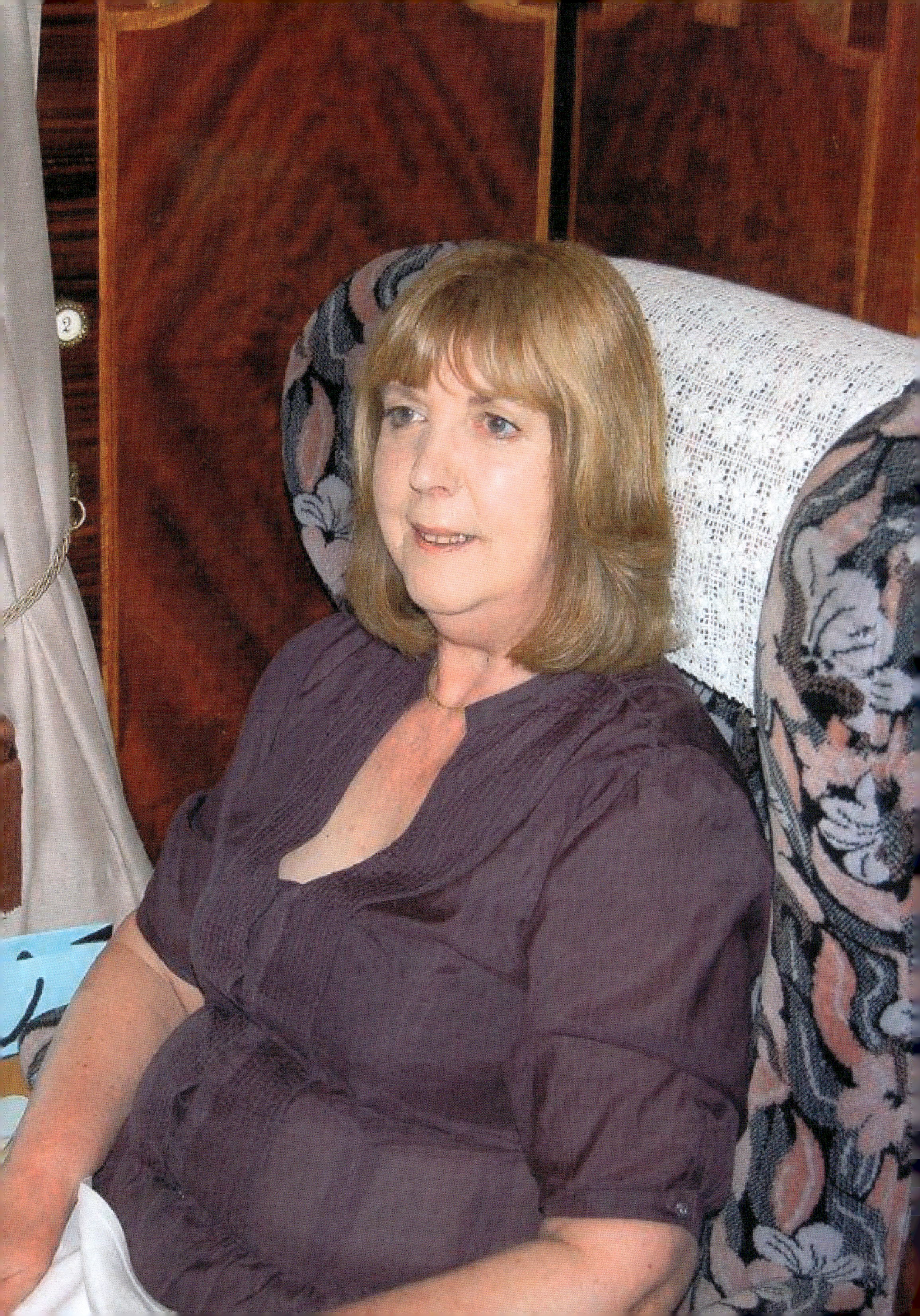

MONICA MUNCH

a moral tale by Mum

This is the story of Monica Munch
Who was too selfish to share her lunch.
If her friends said *Monica, give us a crisp!*
She would disappear like the will o'the wisp.

One day in the playground
She opened her satchel
And found she'd forgotten to put in her apple.
She told her friends of her unhappy plight... But
they wouldn't even give her one bite.

So, if you want to keep friends...
...And also eat lunch:
Don't behave like Monica Munch!

JACK'S HOMEWORK

Jack got commended by the visiting poet, Mick Gowar - and passed on the congratulations when she got home.

The doorknob rattles
The floorboards creak
Someone's there
But no one speaks.
Ghostly shadows
On the wall
Shadows that aren't there at all...

*Someone's in this room of mine
Sending shivers down my spine.*

Across my face
A brush of fur
And then I hear
A welcome purr.
No ghost is this!
No need to fear!
Mistoffelees my cat is here.

Mum, 1983

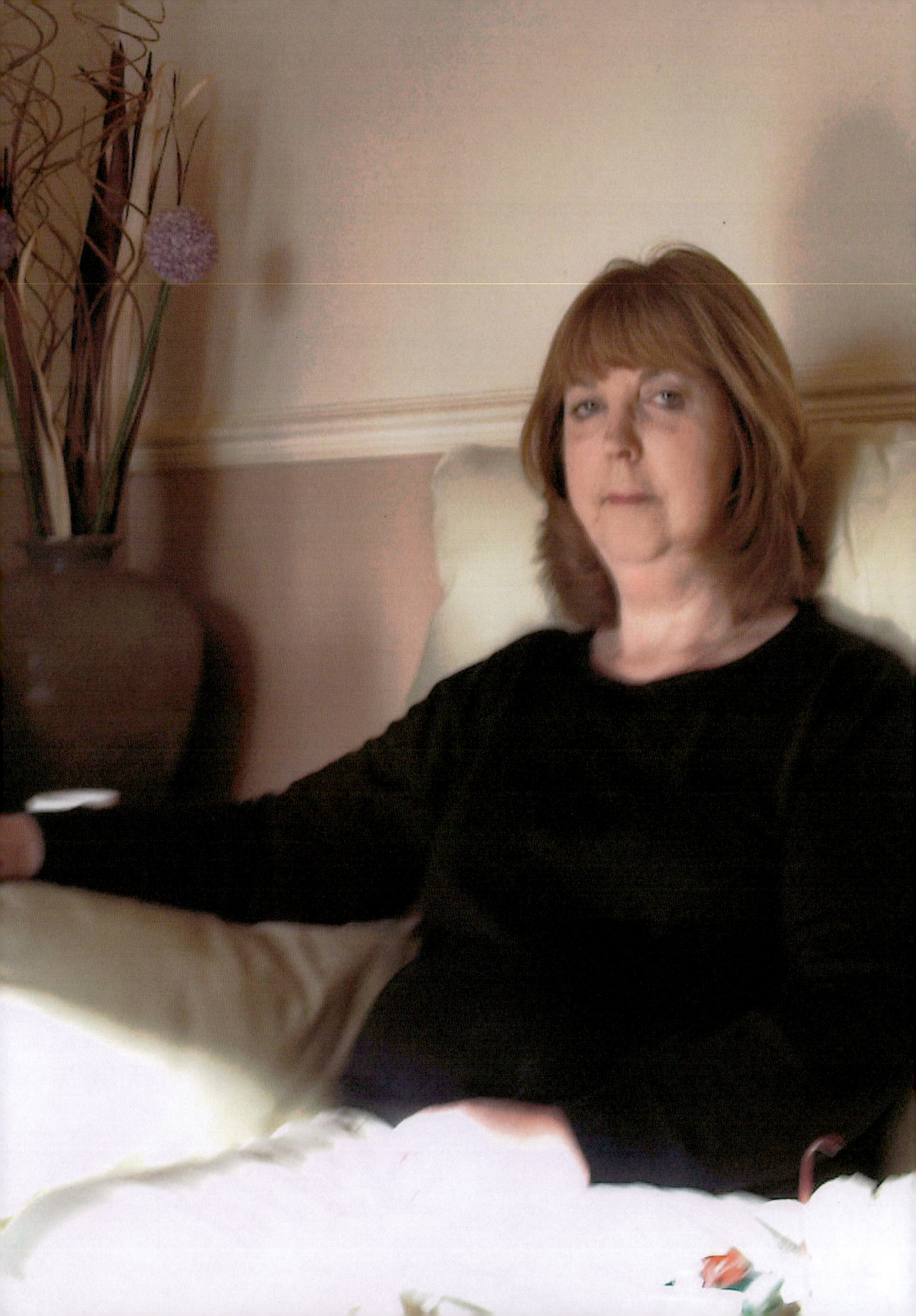

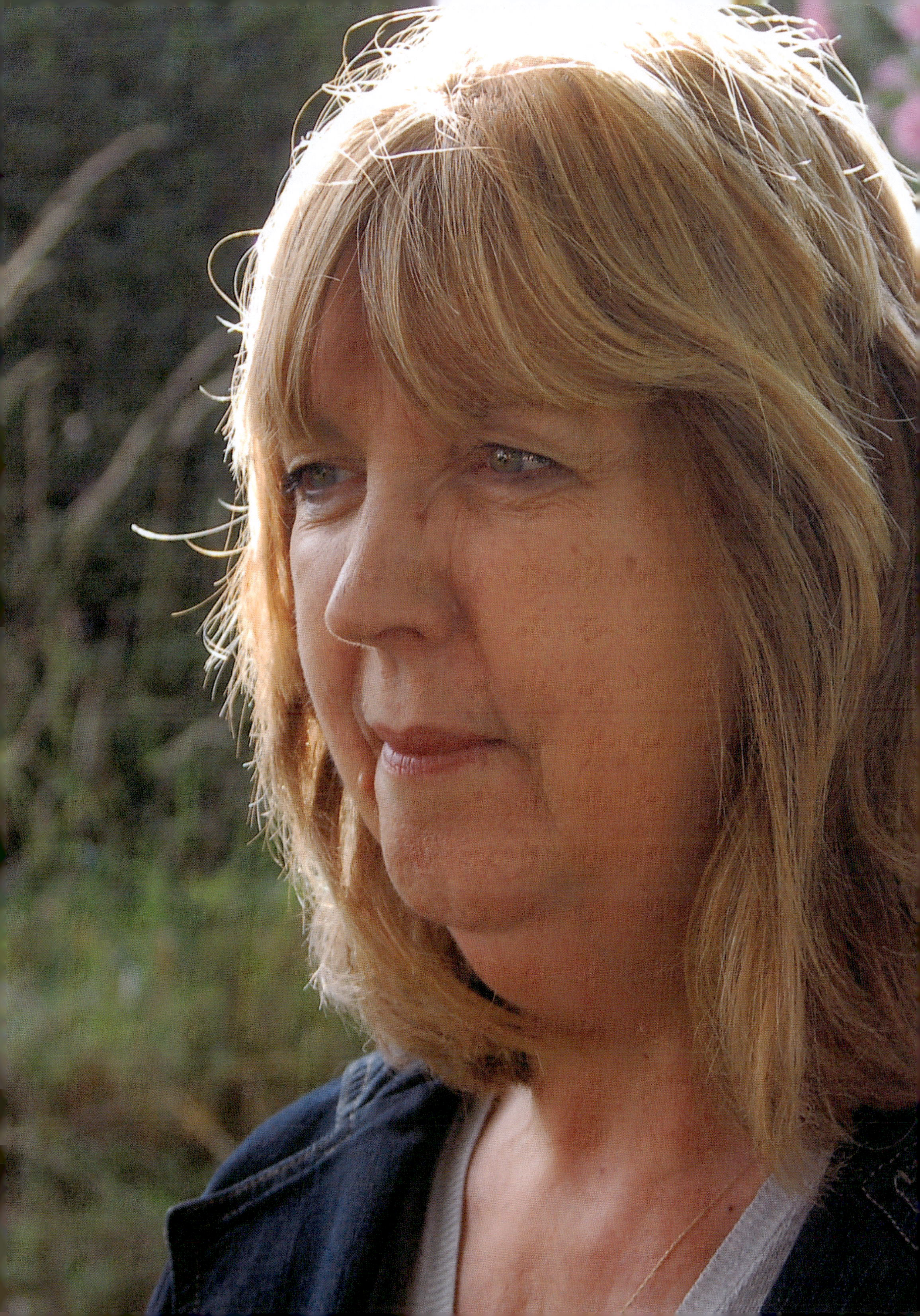

MOTHER

You know, I think it's your eyes! I was sitting here wondering how to start writing and every time I thought of your qualities as a mother – wisdom, calm, perspective, patience, kindness, omniscience, generosity, depth, grace, groundedness, selflessness, humour, being there, homeliness, beauty, gentleness, perceptiveness, strength – I saw it all in your eyes. As you use them to look through this book, I hope you will see it too… and then you'll understand why and how you mean so much.

Mum and Dad are my base. Number 17's where I can remember who I am. Mum carries this power around inside her…so that I feel happy and whole regardless of whether I'm on the settee with a cup of tea asking her if she watched *Walter Presents* the night before, or in the car bombarding her with unwelcome analyses of the lyrics playing on Radio 2, or in a pub or garden centre ordering two diet cokes (one without ice), or on holiday with three young boys, admiring her ability to create order from chaos, a home from home, and wetting ourselves (Mum and I, not the young boys) with laughter at just about everything and nothing.

While I'm there, a holiday in Scarborough in 2007ish provides an example of her quiet patience and stoicism. I'd thought that we hadn't been leaving the accommodation (a WW1 barrack hut) until about noon each day because we were enjoying the relaxed pace and digesting our French toasts. Turns out she was giving the new bottle of Bio-Oil I was putting on my face at nine o'clock every morning a chance to lose its wet gleam before being seen in public with me. She patiently waited until the last day before telling me.

In 1980 I saw a blue furry hippo in Luton Arndale's "Taylor & McKenna" toy shop and couldn't get him out of my mind. A week later Mum took me to buy him. It was a magical purchase – Peepers actually went with me everywhere for years after – and I have a really vivid memory of standing on the Bute Street station platform looking down at his face in the branded white paper bag and feeling so frightened that I'd drop him in the gap as I boarded the train. I said as much to Mum as the train pulled up and she smiled at me with her Cupid's bow, *Winter Wine* lips and her dark green eyes and said, "I know!" She knew. She knew everything. She knew me and how I was feeling. I felt the power of love, empathy and security.

In *Sons & Lovers*, D.H. Lawrence writes of the main character that, "nothing had happened in his life until he'd told it to his mother". That's exactly it! Ask my boys how many times a day I say "Remind me to tell Grandma". She IS my life!

Many Happy Returns of the Day Mooti! Love ya! Jacqueline xxx

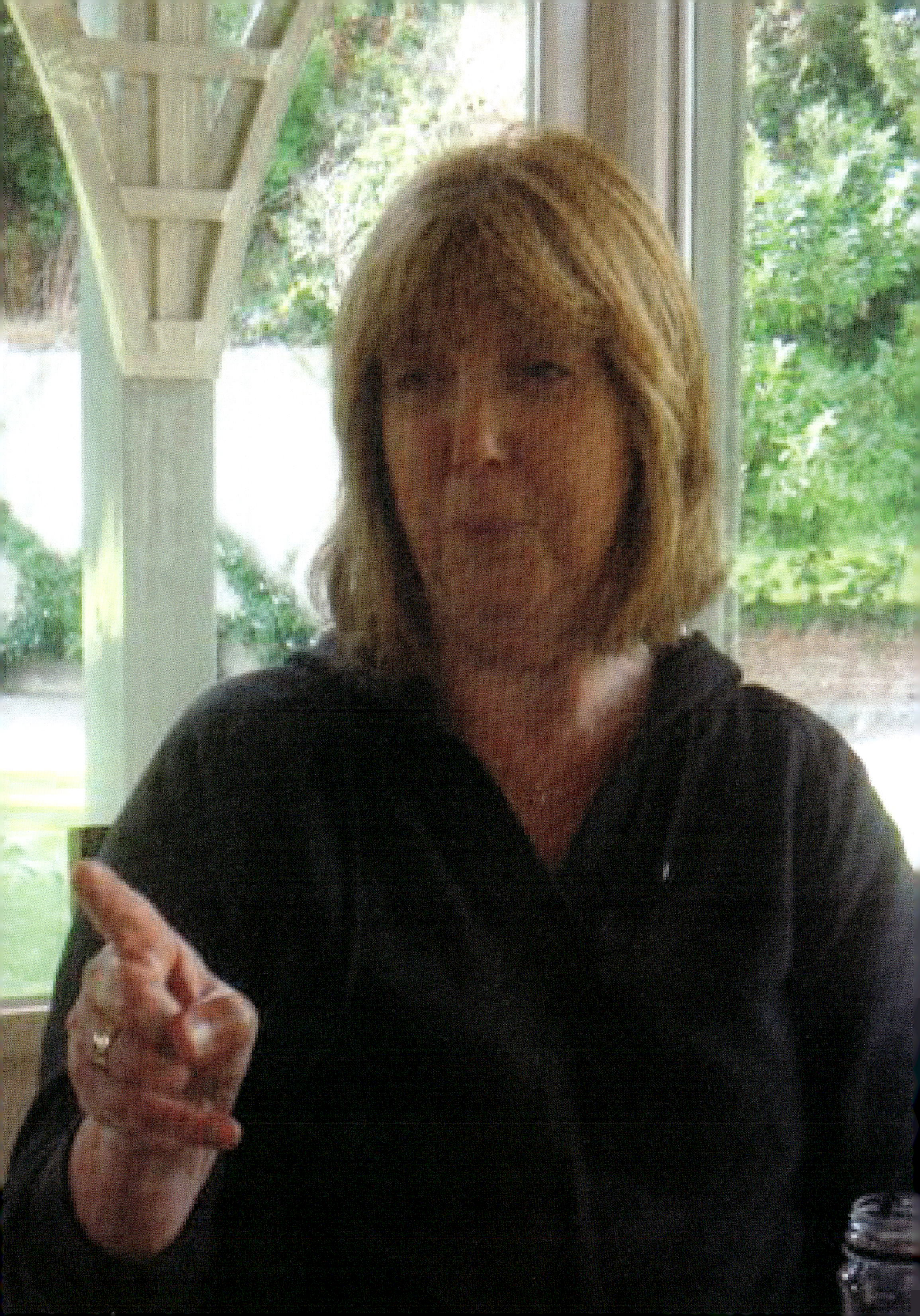

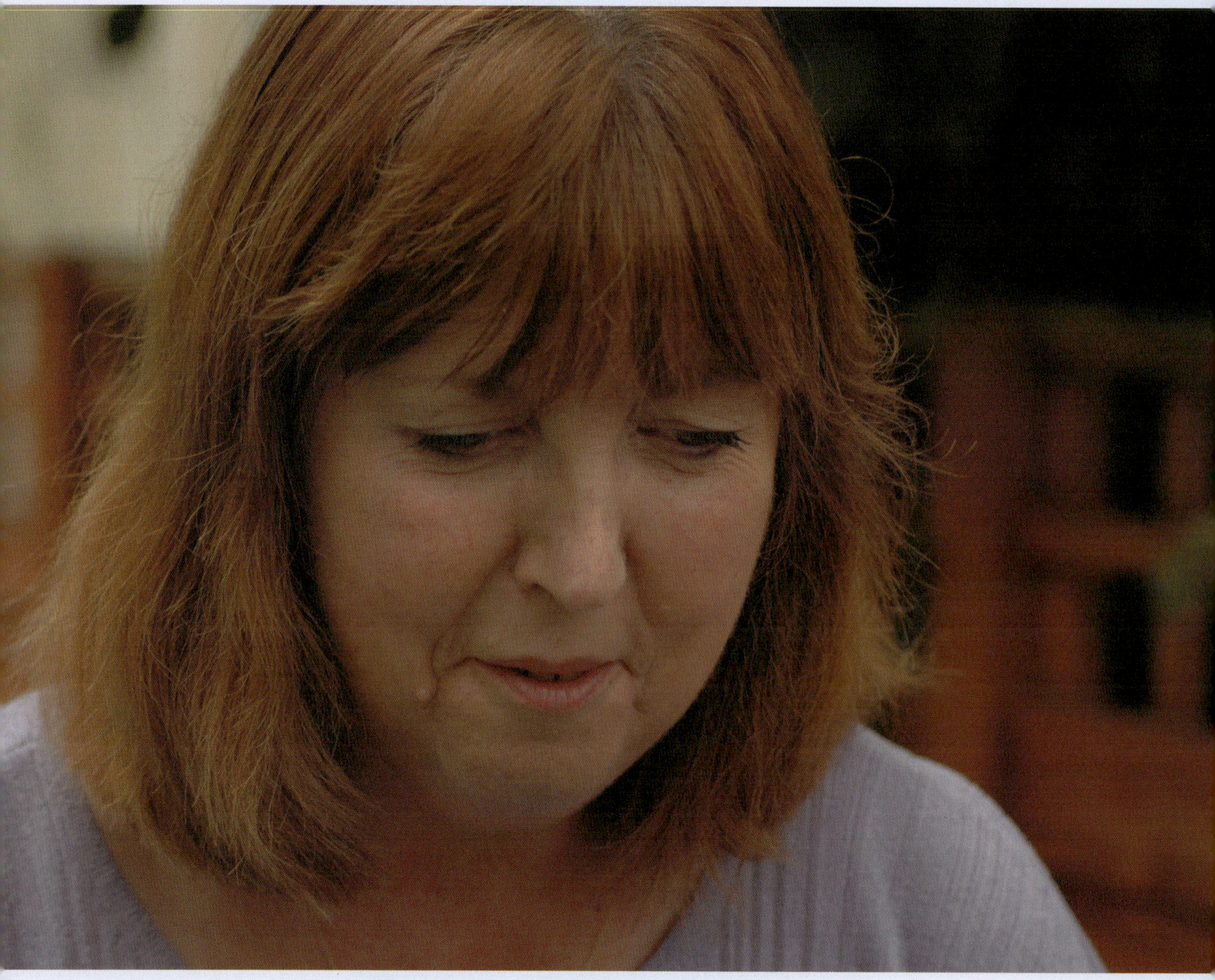

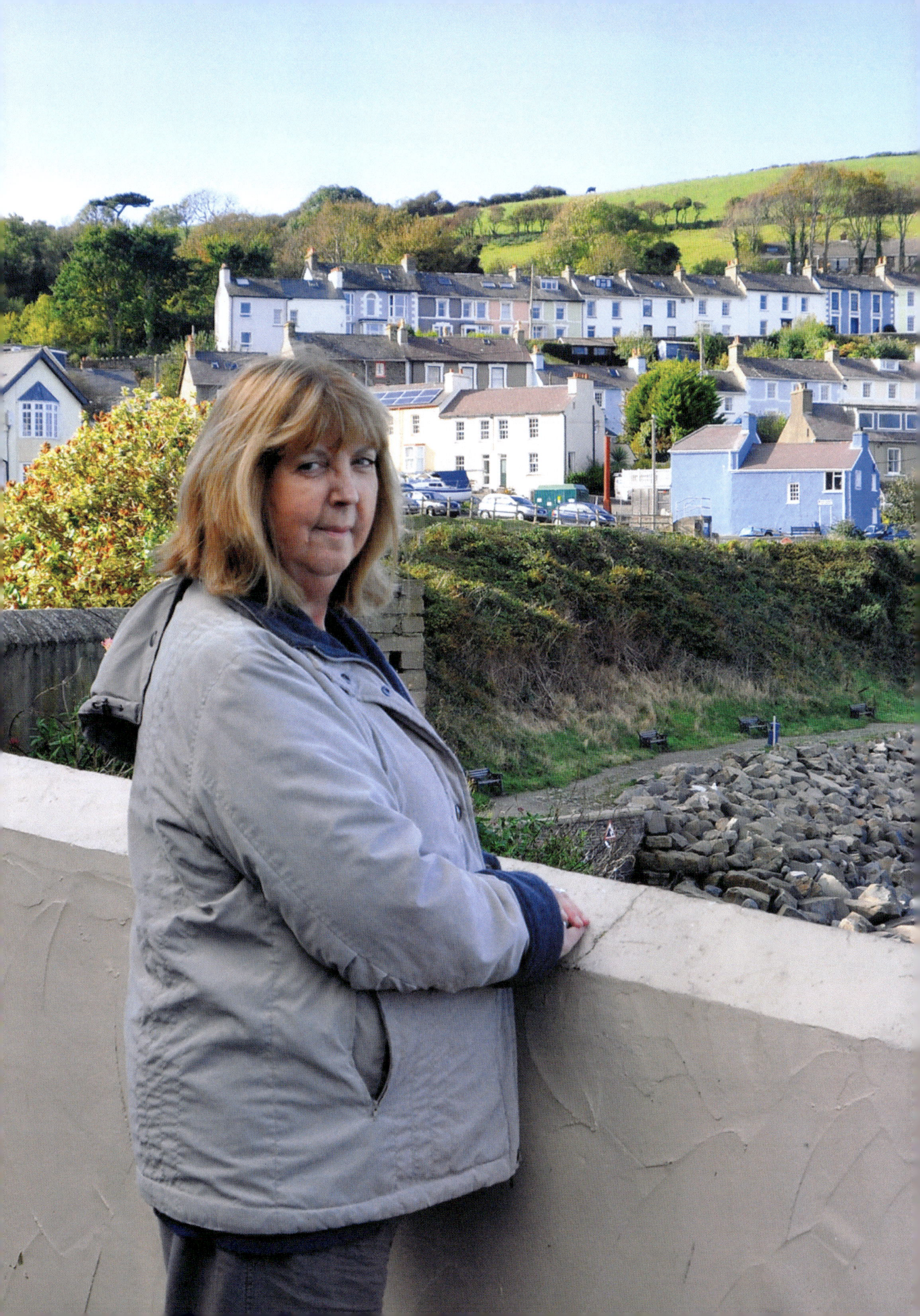

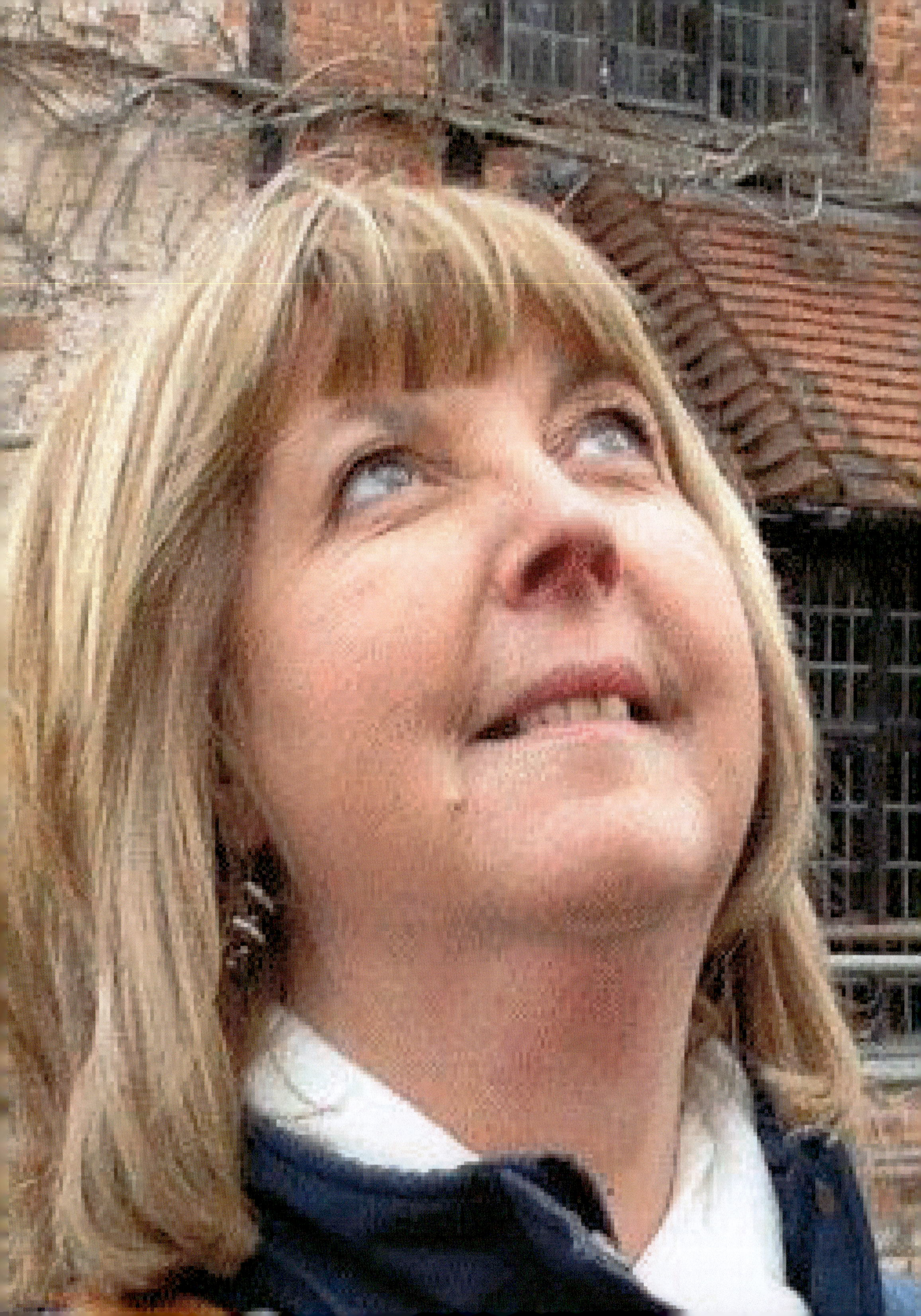

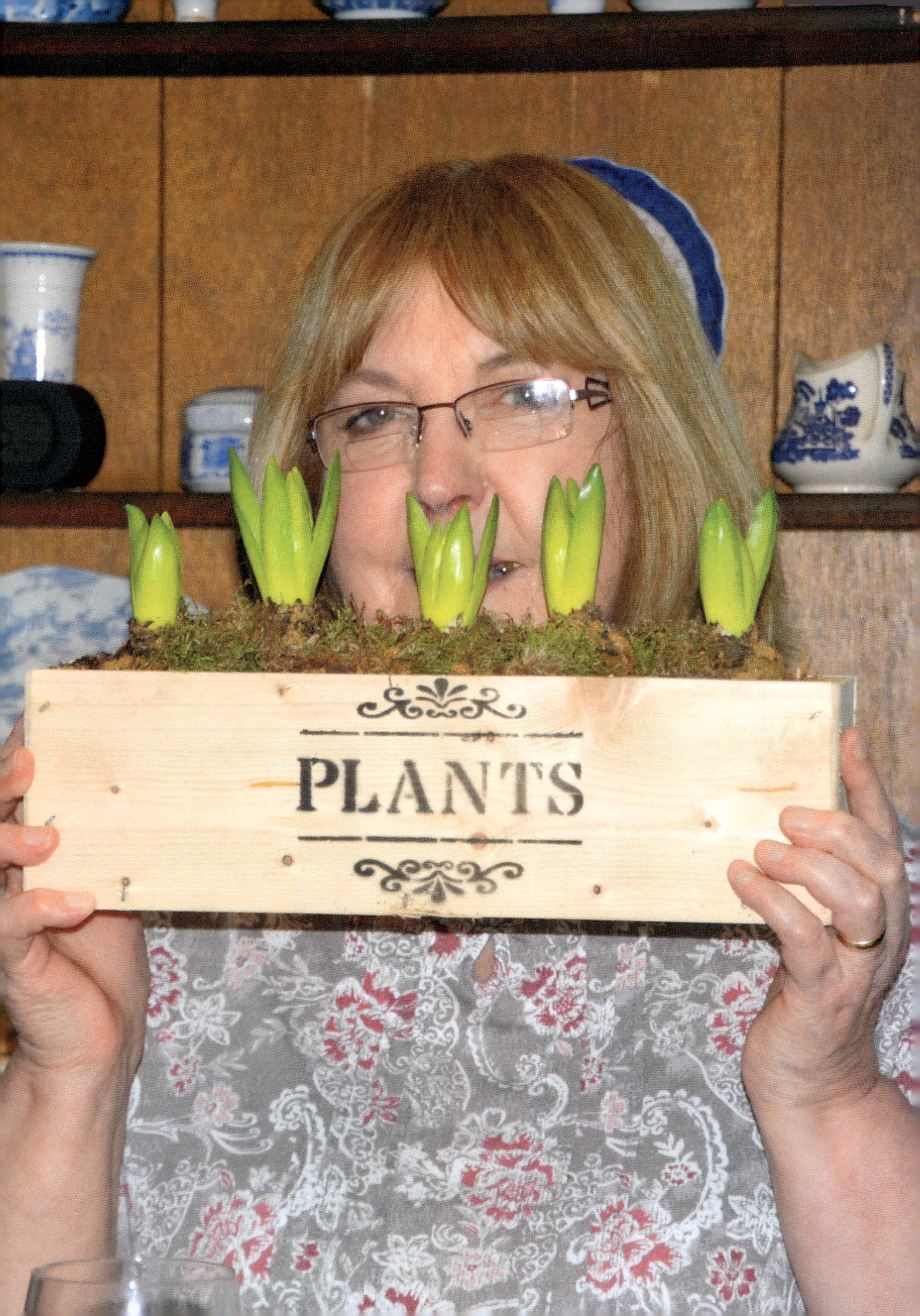
PLANTS

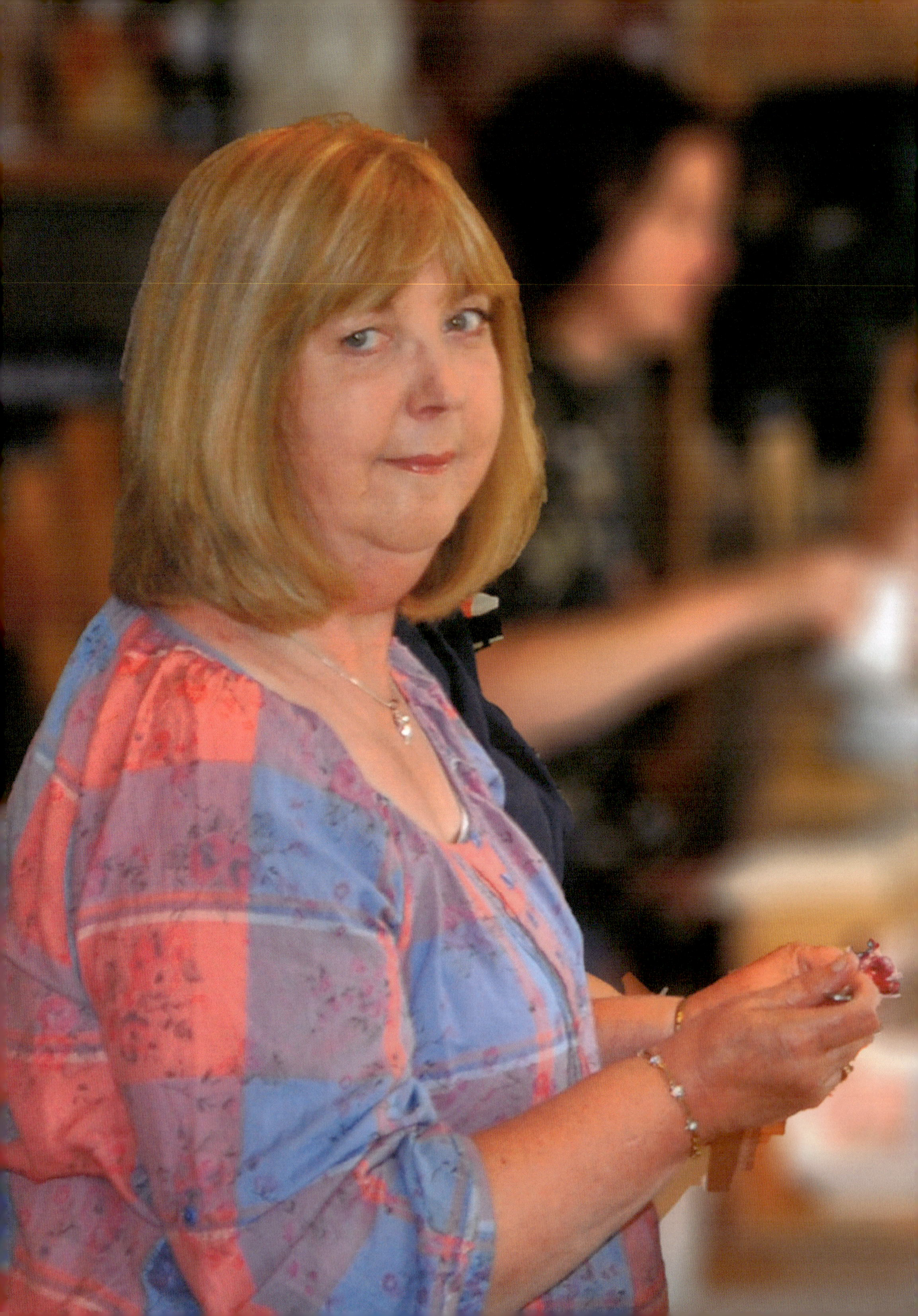

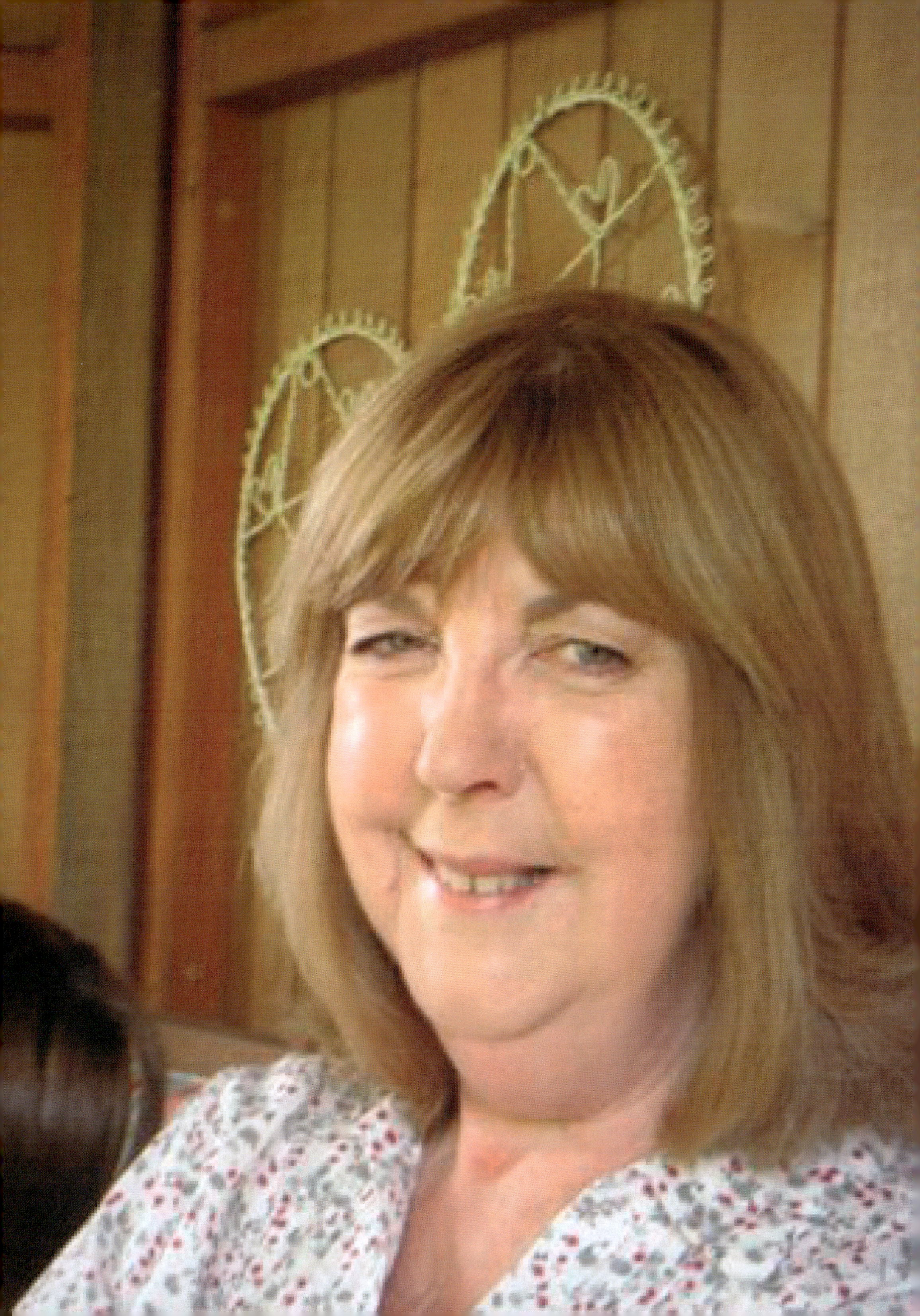

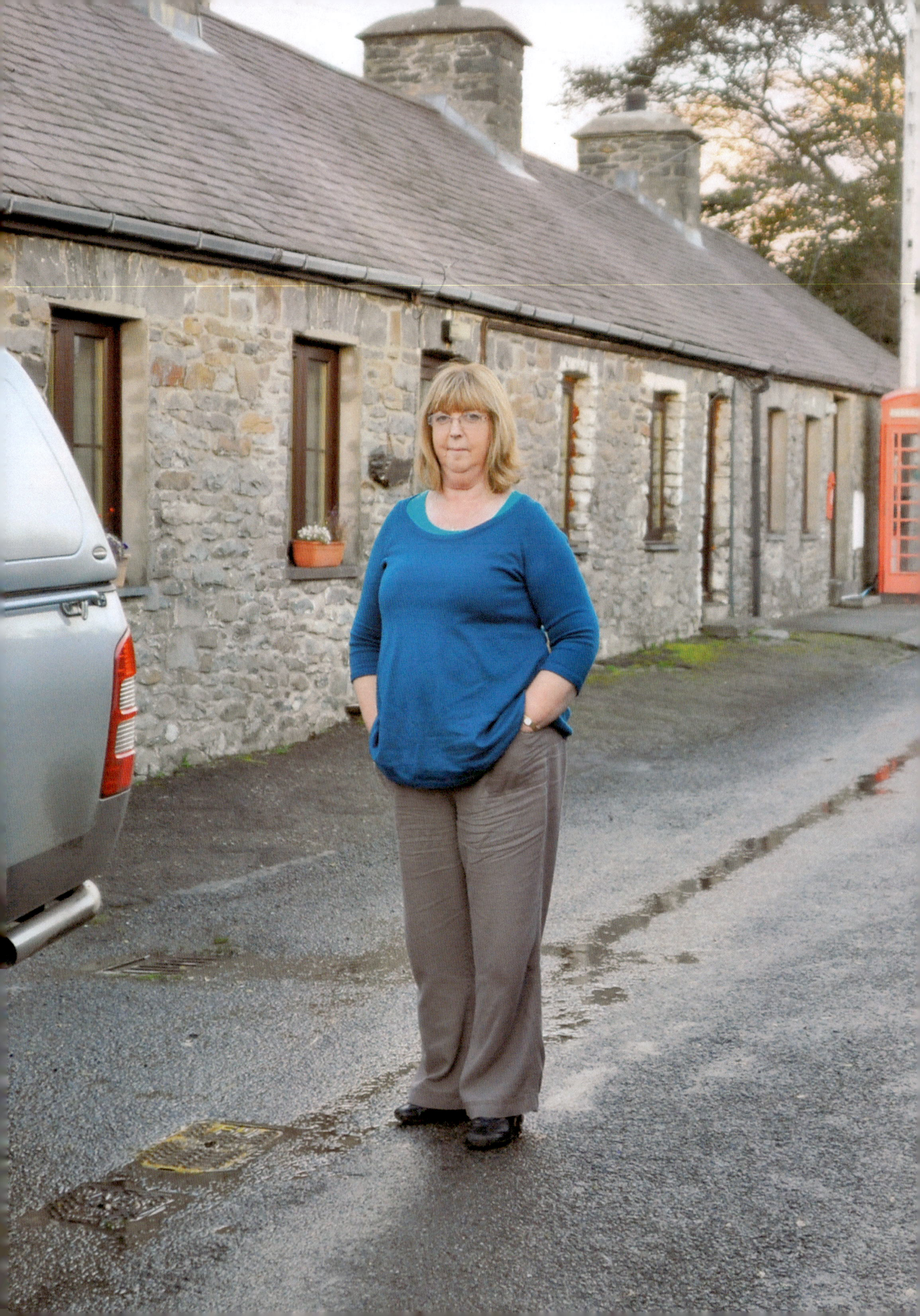

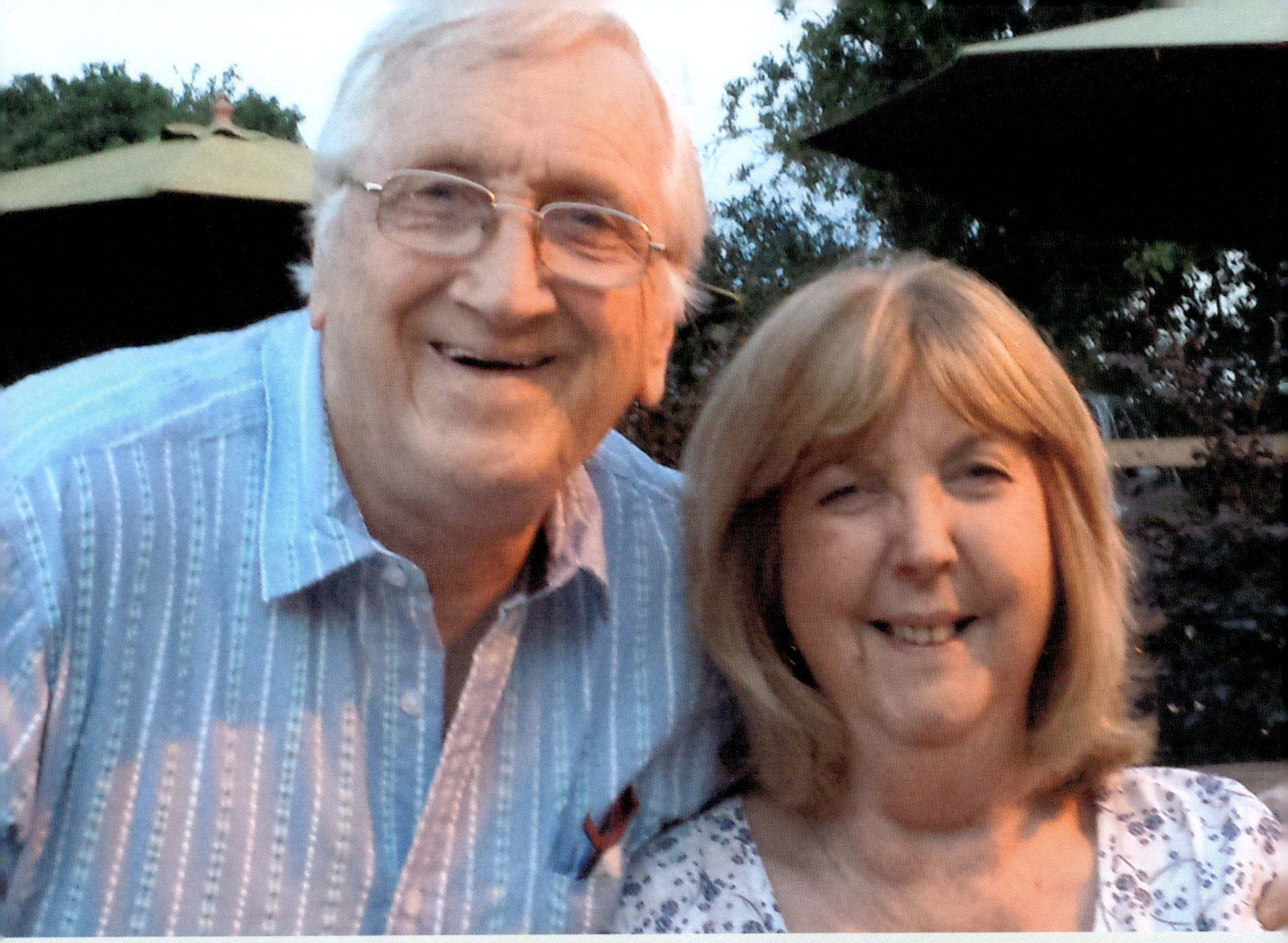

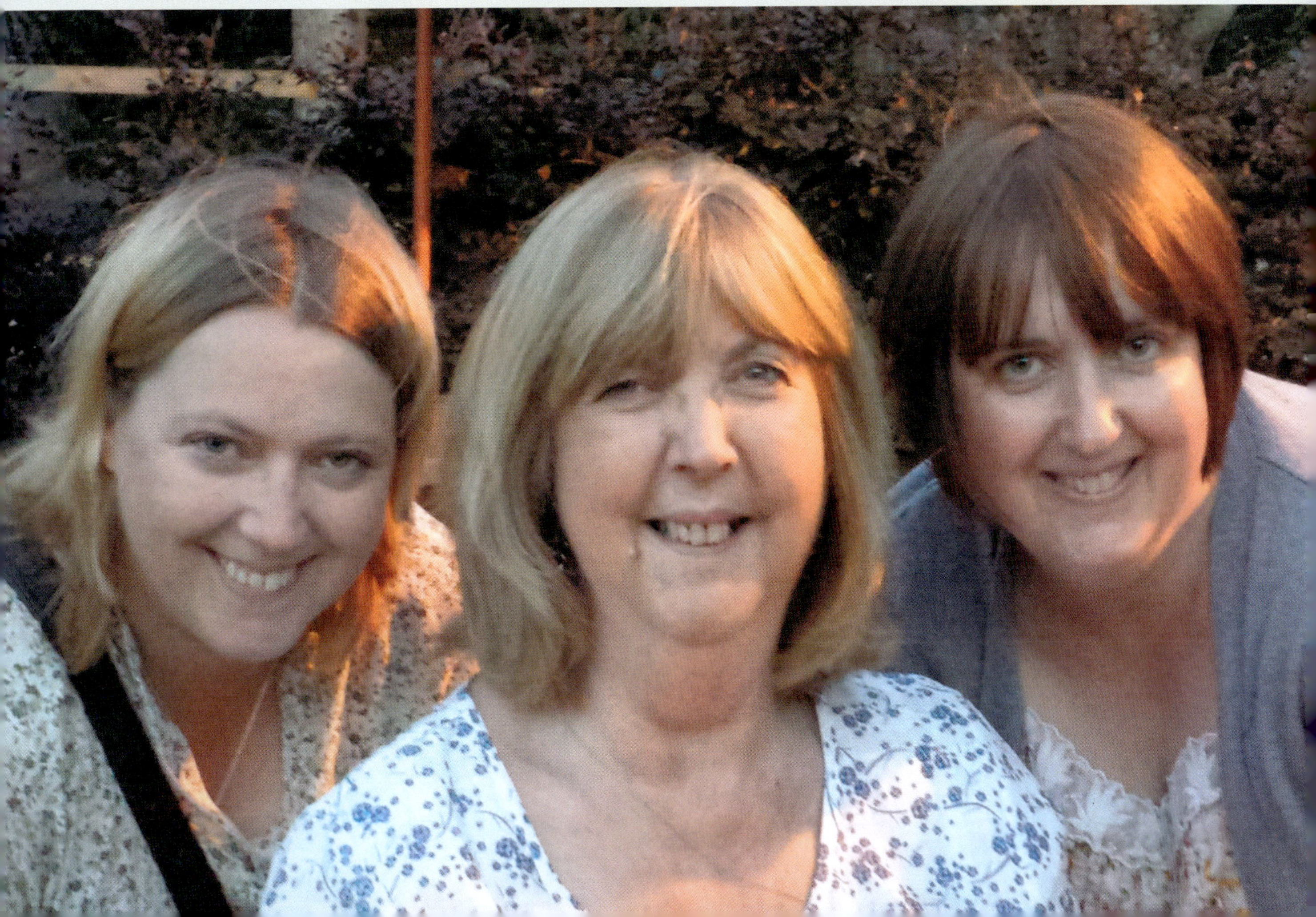

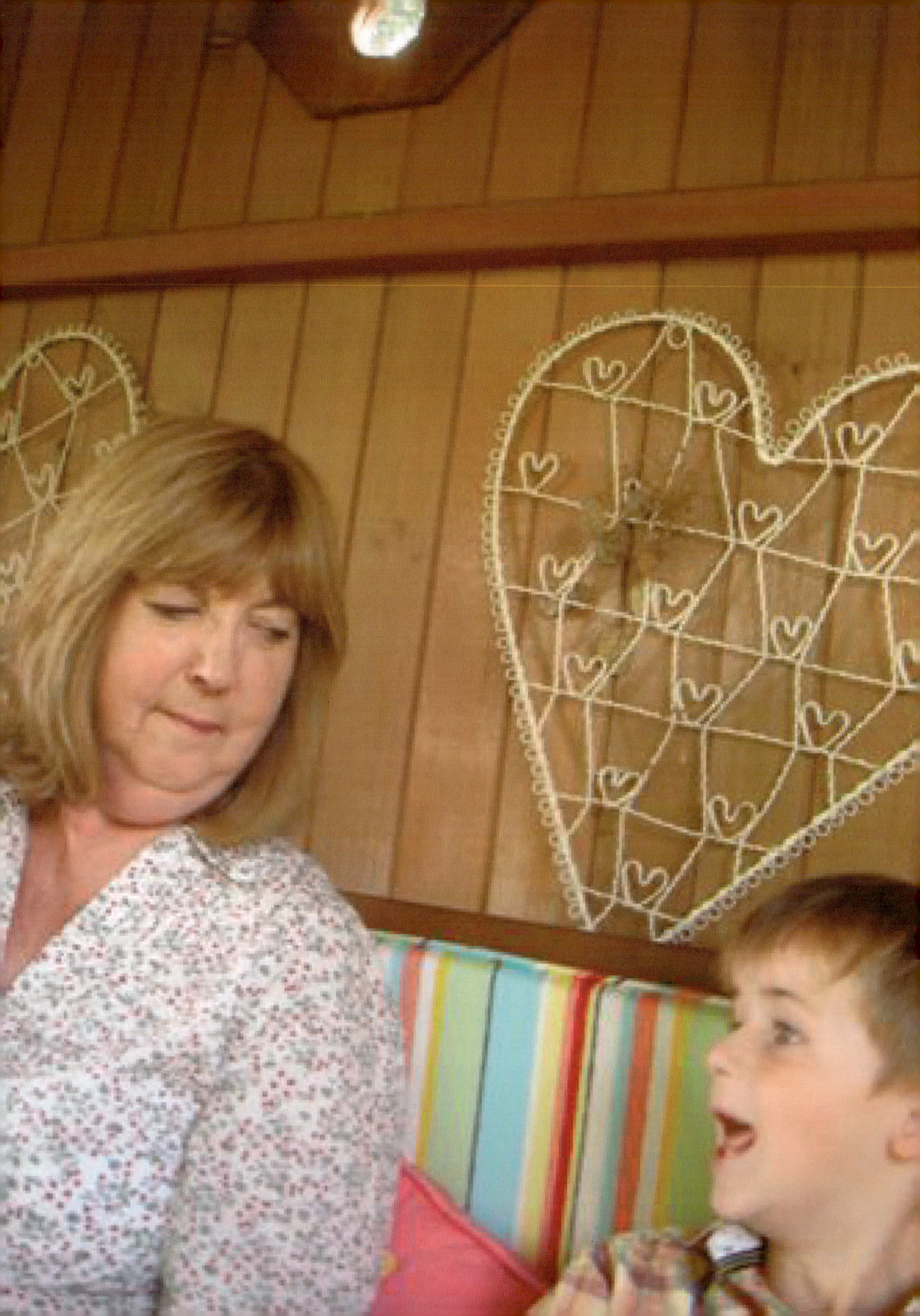

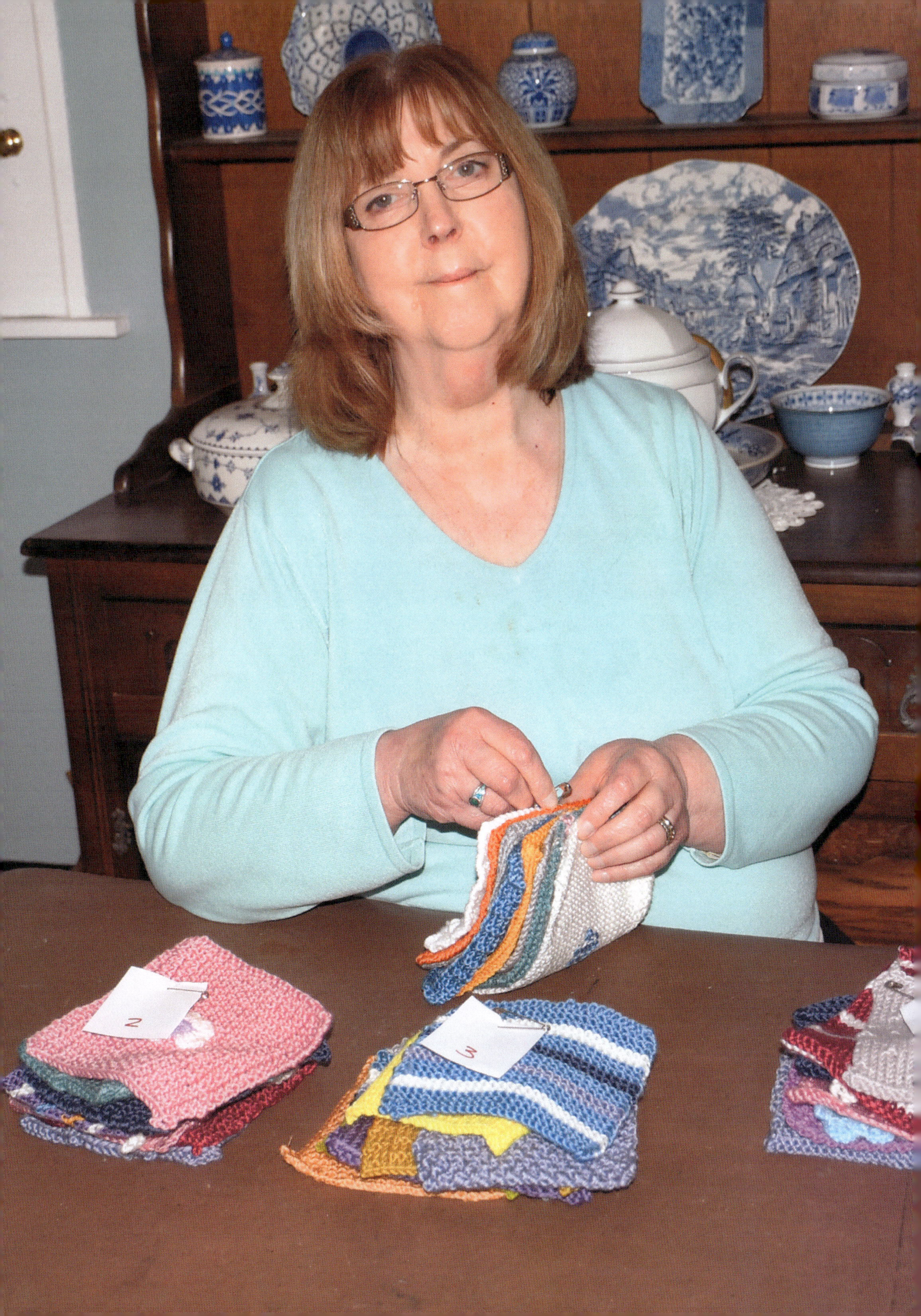
2
3

GRANDMA

Grandma, when I first met you in Bedford Hospital's maternity ward on the 13th December 1998, a date that has never left me, I thought there must have been a mistake, so young you looked. It was only on seeing Grandpa, looking a respectable 40, that this key fact, you both being my grandparents, formed completely in the vegetable soup of my infant brain. Even now, 23 years on, I have cause for skepticism but second third and fourth opinions all confirm that you simply have not aged. Nonetheless it is your eightieth. Some aspects of you confirm this, your liking for Tom Jones growing more conspicuous by the day in a world which hás seen X Factor come and go; while others, like your laugh, your eyes, and your sense of style, are as fresh as ever. I feel immensely lucky to have had you feature so prominently in my life, while so many people whose grandparents are too geographically or temperamentally removed from them cannot say the same. Even if you don't realise it you're the absolute lynchpin of the family, and I am not alone in my boundless love for and gratitude to you. Enjoy your birthday safe in the knowledge that you've more than enriched the lives of everyone who has had the privilege of knowing and loving you.

Your grandson James

Happy birthday Grandma.
Thanks for providing me with hundreds of toffees and squirty cream and being there for all my fake school sick days. Also for stopping me from going insane.

Love you lots!! George

Dear Grandma,
I'll never forget falling over accidentally on purpose to get a magic sweet or the time you took us go karting in Westward Ho! while Mum was dying of food poisoning.
   Thanks for always being present and having something apt to share, whether it's some of your endless wisdom or one of your captivating stories, from seeing The Beatles to having an anonymous hedgehog donor. Thanks for your unconditional love and for being the best grandma in the world.

Love from Hugh

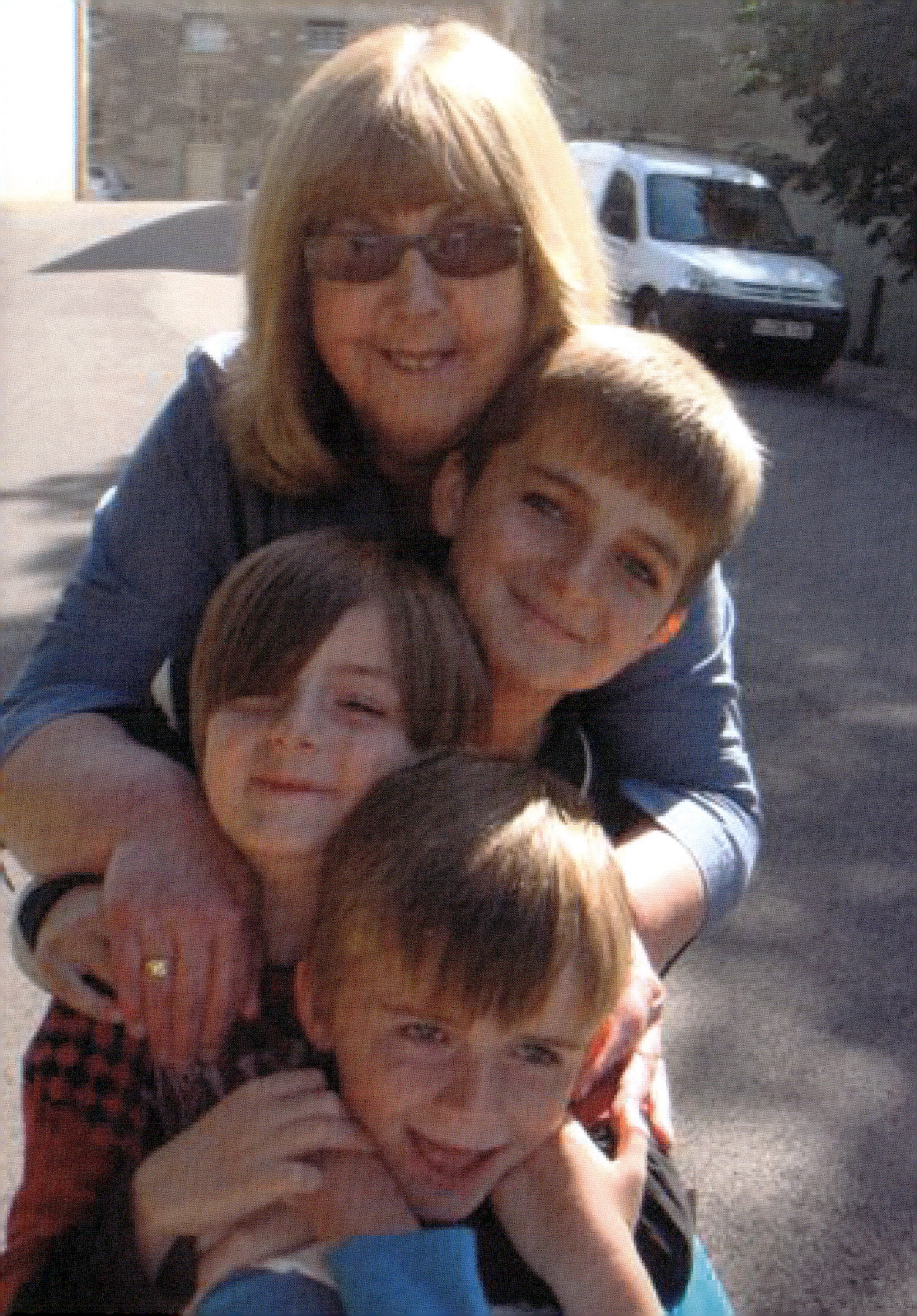

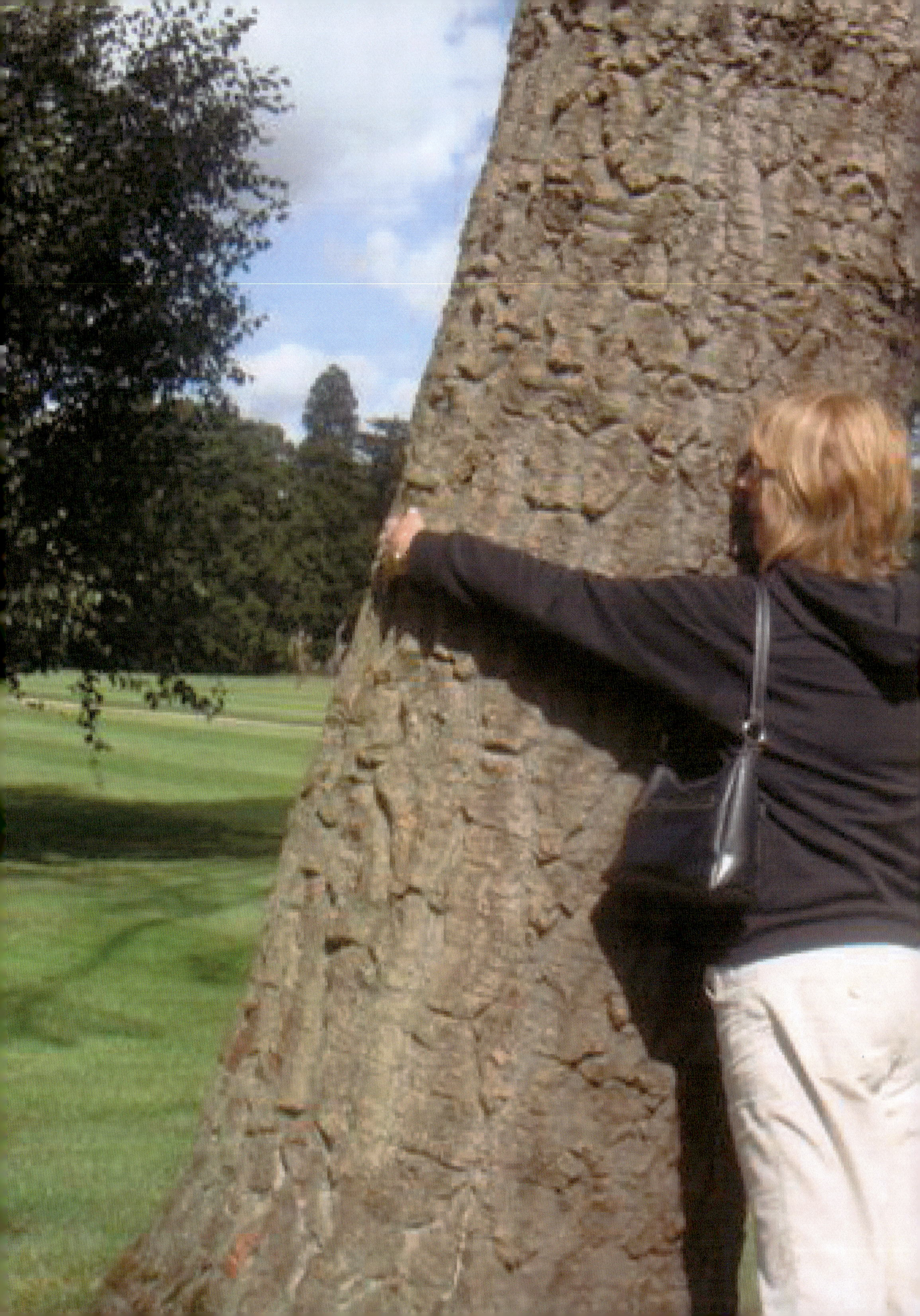

Most photos by Peter Davies. (Obviously not this tree-hugging one.)

Printed in Great Britain
by Amazon